STEP by STEP
KARATE
SKILLS

Dan Bradley

Specially
commissioned
photographs by
Mike O'Neill

HAMLYN

Dedication
To Beth

Acknowledgements

Photographs
Front and back jacket: Mike O'Neill

All photographs by Mike O'Neill except the following:
Sylvio Dekov: pages 13, 83, 95, 107, 113, 121

Artwork Mei Lim

The author and publisher would like to thank:

Vic Charles, World Heavyweight Champion, for contributing the Champion's Tips. Vic also appears in some of the photographs

Jack Warner, of the Amateur Shotokan Karate Association, for his advice and assistance

Barney Whelan, Chairman of the British Karate Federation, who sanctioned this book

Brian Smith, English Chief Referee, for his explanation of the competition rules

Dr Jim Canney, WUKO medical adviser and British team doctor, for his medical and health advice

The photographic models: Colin Hexley, Jennie Sanders, Tony Cooper, Manjit Gosal and Fiona Cooper, for their expertise and patience

Rose Clark, who typed the manuscript

Note
In the instructional photographs, the initiator of an attack is wearing a red belt and the opponent a white belt. This is to facilitate identification and also to follow competition regulations

Published by
The Hamlyn Publishing Group Limited
Bridge House, 69 London Road
Twickenham, Middlesex TW1 3SB
and distributed for them by
Octopus Distribution Services
Rushden, Northamptonshire

First published in 1987

ISBN 0 600 50350 X

Printed in Italy

CONTENTS

FOREWORDS

BY THE CHAIRMAN OF THE BRITISH KARATE FEDERATION

Karate has recently been accepted into the Olympic movement and I am very happy to commend this book on competition karate. Written with the younger karate enthusiast in mind, it is well presented, structured for easy and progressive learning and is extremely well illustrated. Dan Bradley is an able and experienced karate instructor and his skills in teaching the techniques of karate are evident in this book. It takes the karate athlete through the basic techniques and shows how they are turned into effective fighting moves. I have no hesitation in recommending it to you as a valuable aid to training in a proper, recognized karate club.

Bernard Whelan
Chairman, British Karate Federation

Coatbridge, Scotland

BY THE PRESIDENT OF THE USA KARATE FEDERATION

The World Union of Karatedo Organizations is the official body representing Karatedo in the Olympic movement. I welcome this book by Dan Bradley. It is up to date on all the competition rules, explains the basic moves and develops them for combat in the competition area. Training methods as well as tactics are described with the accompanying photographs being particularly helpful. I am happy to recommend this book for the aspiring students to use as a reference and for ideas as they go through their training programme.

George E Anderson 8th Dan
First Vice President, World Union of Karatedo Organizations
President, Pan American Union of Karatedo Organizations
President, The US Karate Federation, Member US Olympic Committee
Past President, World Referee Council, WUKO

Akron, Ohio
USA

TAKE CARE

Karate is a combat sport and the techniques described in this book are potentially dangerous, the more so if performed unsupervised. Practise only under the guidance of a qualified coach or instructor. The author and the publisher cannot accept responsibility for any injury resulting from practising the karate moves described in this book.

ABOUT THE AUTHOR

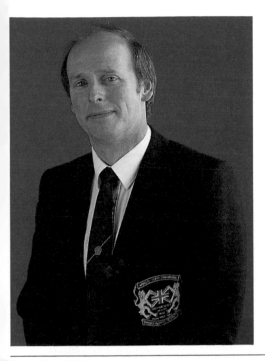

Dan Bradley is Chairman of the English Karate Council and Vice Chairman of the British Karate Federation, the officially-recognized bodies for karate in Britain. He regularly attends major national and international karate events and is well-versed in all aspects of competition karate. Fluent in several languages, he is an astute and respected international karate politician. He referees in both *kata* and *kumite*. With some 25 years' experience in karate and martial arts, he holds a black belt fourth dan in *shotokan* karate and is a qualified coach. In addition to writing this book, he contributes items to sports magazines and advises the BBC World Service on karate.

VIC CHARLES' CAREER HIGHLIGHTS

World Heavyweight Champion 1986
World Games Openweight Champion 1981/85
World Cup Heavyweight Champion 1987
European Openweight Champion 1981/82
European Heavyweight Champion 1984
Television 'Superstars' All-round winner 1981
English Heavyweight Champion 1978/79/81/82/84/85/86
Member of British World Champions Team 1982/86

The Champion's Tips are contributed by Vic Charles

INTRODUCING KARATE

The beginning of karate
Karate originated about a thousand years ago as a means of self-defence and attacking an aggressor. It began with a Buddhist monk, Bhodidharma, from what is now northern India. He migrated to China where he taught the monks in the temples of Shaolin various exercises designed to strengthen their bodies so that they could withstand the harsh regime of monastic life.

Those exercises which he devised all those years ago were very similar to the modern day karate techniques which you can see in any karate *dojo* (training hall) in any part of the world.

The techniques spread slowly by word of mouth and by secret practice to the island of Okinawa (part of the Ryuku Islands, now owned by their northerly neighbour, Japan), where in feudal times the peasantry were not allowed to carry weapons. To defend themselves against the cruel war lords the peasants resorted to the ancient exercises of Bhodidharma and refined them into unarmed punching, chopping and kicking methods which through practice became lethal techniques in themselves when employed by experts.

Sport karate
This art then spread further to Japan where it was adopted and developed in the 1930s by Gichin Funakoshi who founded a formal training programme for this new martial art, which he called karate – which means literally 'empty hand'. After a slow start in Japan this martial art became very popular in Europe and the USA after the second world war.

Since the mid-1970s karate has gained several million practitioners and has now developed into sport karate, which bans the most dangerous techniques but retains the power and speed of the original martial art.

Karate's acceptance into the Olympic movement in 1986 has further improved its status and world-wide appeal. It is now an exciting and spectacular combat sport which requires hard practice and much self-control in training and competition.

This book tells you how to learn and perform the competition techniques used in karate, how to block and counter attack and finally how to employ tactics and strategies to defeat your opponent.

Who can do karate?
Karate can be practised by anyone of any age. Clearly if you are, say, middle-aged or haven't been doing any sport recently, it would be advisable to obtain a clearance from your doctor first. As with any sport there's a risk of injury or sudden illness, perhaps more so in karate where the body has to take lots of knocks and shocks.

However, the sport can be, and is, adapted very easily to the needs of anyone who wishes to learn its skills. There are physically handicapped people who train under a programme prepared for them to cater for their particular disabilities.

The attraction of karate for many people is that it isn't necessary to keep having competitions against others. Competition is optional in almost all karate clubs and so anyone who wishes to become fit and learn the karate techniques without having to enter regular competitions can do so.

Karate for children
Karate is very popular among children. Parents naturally want their offspring to develop self-confidence, grow up fit and healthy and at the same time be able to look after themselves.

Children are taught a modified form of karate which prohibits head and face attacks and concentrates more on performing techniques properly and developing self-control. Any sparring or competition which they do is strictly supervised and their safety is paramount.

Children have soft bones and undeveloped muscles and care must be taken to avoid damaging them. Ten years is a reasonable age for a child to start karate but much depends on factors such as the maturity of the child, the attitude of the club coach etc. An instructor should always obtain written permission from parents for a child to train in karate.

Find a good club

This book describes what you need to do to become a competitor in sport karate. You can't learn karate just from a book, however. You have to find a good club with a competent coach, who understands not only his sport but also the needs and aspirations of his students. Make sure that the coach and club are properly licensed and insured and that they are recognized by the official ruling body. Ensure that the club offers what you want. You are the consumer paying your fees and the modern karate club must give value for money.

The lynchpin of a good club is a good coach. A competent coach will run a happy hard-working karate club. A good coach should welcome you on your first visit to his club. He will be a member of an officially recognized body or association. He'll be able to tell you how much it will cost to train and to buy a karate suit, explain the cost of a karate licence or a training permit, give you details of his own insurance cover and will explain what insurance you'll need to train safely and without worry.

Look at the premises. Is the training area free from obstacles? Is it big enough? Is the floor safe? Is it slippery, too solid? Are mats available for competition training? Be wary of a karate instructor who tries to rush you into parting with your money or who tries to fob off your inquiry about insurance cover and safety of his students.

Finally, don't visit just one club, but have a look at several to see what sort of training and atmosphere appeal to you. There are different styles of karate and perhaps one will be more attractive to you than others.

What you need

A beginner in karate should obtain a karate licence at an early stage. As well as giving a *karateka* (practitioner of karate) official recognition, a licence also gives a measure of insurance cover against injury in training. Injuries can occur at all levels of karate practice, so it is advisable to take out a licence as soon as possible after beginning training.

You will also need to buy a karate suit, or *gi*, once you have decided to continue training after your first couple of lessons. You can buy karate suits in sports shops but your instructor may well be able to advise you where to buy a good reasonably-priced suit.

The risk of injury

Karate has often been compared with boxing by those who don't really understand the concept of sport karate, but there is a fundamental difference between these two combat sports. In boxing the object of the exercise is to punch your opponent's head as hard as you can so that his brain is injured and he collapses into unconsciousness.

Karate on the other hand, while including attacks to the head with punches and kicks, disallows full contact to the head. In competition a head attack may make only the slightest skin touch: anything more heavy is penalized. A serious infringement will be penalized with immediate disqualification.

It's difficult to acquire the skill to 'pull' a punch or a kick sufficiently to score a point and yet not make excessive contact. For this reason novices are not encouraged to try head attacks until their timing and focusing ability is sufficiently developed.

With punches to the body actual contact has to be made to score a point, but again the force used must be controlled. With regular training you will find that your control improves and at the same time your body becomes better able to absorb heavy punches and kicks.

Styles of karate

Competition and sport karate have universal rules for scoring points and match behaviour. There are several different styles of karate which you can practise which are compatible with these competition rules. The four most common styles are *Shotokan* (which has long and low stances and powerful techniques), *Wado ryu* (a fast style with upright stances), *Shukokai* (noted for its powerful punches), *Goju ryu* (a traditional style noted for the bodily strength of its practitioners).

All karate styles require hard practice and no one style is better or worse than another. No one style of karate tends to produce more champions than other styles. What style you do will depend probably on what appeals to you personally or whatever style your local club practises.

The importance of discipline and respect

As karate is potentially a dangerous sport, self-control and discipline in training are very important. Partners training together have to be absolutely sure of each other's control and intentions, otherwise serious injury could result. Karate is founded on

1:1
Rei: standing bow

1:2
Yoi: relaxed but alert

discipline and this is a thread which runs through all aspects of the sport. The coach's commands must be instantly and correctly obeyed. This aspect of karate is a valuable asset in character building.

Respect for everyone is another attribute which karate teaches. Respect for colleagues, instructor and for lower grades is essential to understand the essence of karate. The ritual bow, called *rei*, is a symbol of this respect.

Photo 1:2 shows the stance called *yoi*, the natural stance awaiting a command. The standing bow is performed by bringing the feet together, hands on thighs and bending the body forward from the hips (photo 1:1).

The *seiza* position is the kneeling posture which features often in karate (photo 1:3); it is used for meditation and relaxation. From the *seiza* position the kneeling bow is performed, as in photo 1:4. Lean the upper body forward and place the palms of your hands on the floor in front of your knees with the fingers pointing inwards. Bring your head down towards the hands but keep your opponent (or the instructor) in view if at all possible. A bow is used at the beginning and the end of any exercise or activity in karate.

Tradition is an essential element in karate. Each school or style has a strong allegiance to its founder and its instructors. All styles of karate share a common respect for each other. The bow is not just an empty gesture. It is a genuine mark of respect for a fellow *karateka*.

On the other hand there should be little mystique or mysticism in karate. A competent karate coach will guide you to proficiency in karate by dint of his experience and ability and through your willingness to work hard and take in what he has to give you.

RED AND WHITE BELTS

In karate competition one fighter wears a red belt, the other a white belt. This is for easy identification. The majority of photographs in this book follow this pattern. In addition it is the red belt who initiates the attacks.

Seiza: kneeling
position

1:4
Kneeling bow

PUNCHES

' Correct punching is fundamental to combat karate. It takes a little time to acquire punching skill, but once you have it you can develop and improve it indefinitely. '

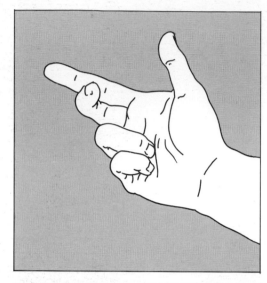

Figure 1
Making a fist: folding the fingers into the palm

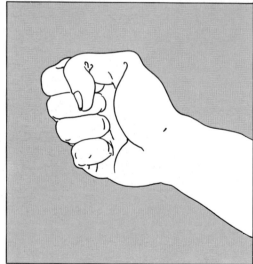

Figure 2
A completed fist: thumb well over, little finger tight

Opposite: A good follow-up punch after a successful foot sweep

To perform karate punches correctly you must first forget many of the popular ideas about punching. The swinging punches so often seen in film and television fiction have nothing to do with the power punching used in karate. Even the punches used in boxing, although similar in some respects, are performed in a different manner from their karate counterparts.

Making a fist
Practise making a first in the following way. Hold your hand out palm upwards. Fold over the little finger into the centre of the palm. Follow it with the next finger, then the

third and the index finger (figure 1). Fit them firmly into the crook of your palm. Then bring over the thumb to lie on top of the index and middle fingers. Now tighten the whole fist and use the leverage of the thumb to keep the fist tight and strong (figure 2). Tighten the fist for five seconds and then relax it but keep the fist closed.

Do this five times, by which time you will be feeling the strain in your lower arm muscles. At this point check the middle of your palms. If they show marks from your finger nails you need to trim the nails.

Don't forget that in all punching practice you should give equal importance to both hands right from your initial training. You will naturally find that you can perform better with one hand than with the other, but equality of skill with both fists is very important and will prove extremely valuable in competition.

Remember also that the attacking fist rotates inwards as it meets its target, while the fist which is being retracted also rotates, but outwards so that it is ready by your side to follow up with another attack if required.

Basic stance for punching
Stand up straight with your feet about shoulder width apart. Point the feet directly forward, not outwards.

Make your right hand into a fist and pull back your right arm so that your upturned fist is resting at the side of your body, just above your hip.

Keep your body upright and make sure that your elbow is pulled back and pointing directly behind you (photo 2:1 overleaf). Your left hand should be pushed straight out in front of you.

The hand may be open before you begin the sequence of punching exercises. If you leave your hand open keep it only slightly open, fingers close together. It should be resting at a point corresponding to the middle of your own, or your imaginary opponent's, chest area.

Make sure that in this stance your body is upright and not off balance.

When you have tried this position several times change the arms round and pull back the left fist leaving the right hand out in front

Right from your early training concentrate fully on your punch. Think about hitting the target. If you let your attention wander your technique will be weak and ineffective.

in what is often called the 'marker' position. That is, theoretically it helps to measure distance and mark your target.

The punching movement

To punch correctly is difficult for the beginner and the technique must be practised slowly at first, gradually building up the complete punch and using the body correctly.

The elements which make up the karate punch include correct arm movement, whiplash tensioning of the muscles in the arm, shoulder, stomach, legs and neck, spot-on timing, proper focusing and total mental commitment to the technique. Clearly, all these factors cannot be mastered at once, so the punch has to be broken down into its several components.

Practise by concentrating on the basic movements, moving on to the use of the muscles, tensioning of the body, then developing the power and timing to produce the ideal karate punch.

To begin, you are standing in the above position, left hand out, right fist drawn back just above your right hip (photo 2:1). Slowly push the right fist forward in a straight line, out and slightly up. Drive it towards the middle of where your opponent's chest would be (photo 2:2). As the fist nears its target rotate it so that it makes its contact with the

thumb underneath, holding the fist in position. The movement should be straight.

The elbow must be kept low and close to the body (photos 2:1 and 2:2). Concentrate on brushing the side of your body with every punching movement. In this way you will avoid the common mistake of letting the elbow come round or up. In karate punching the elbow in general stays behind the punching fist and acts as a driving force, as if it were a piston thrusting all its power along the cylinder that is the punch's line of attack.

The other hand

While the right hand is making its attack the left hand has an equally important job to do. It must compensate for the power and forward thrust generated by the attacking right fist. It does this by pulling back in a straight line as the right fist comes forward.

As the attacking fist reaches its target the left hand should have become a fist and should be settling at the left side of the body just above the hip, in a position corresponding to that made by the right fist immediately before the attacking move.

You can start this alternating movement quite slowly, with no power but trying to align the two movements so that they start and finish simultaneously. A useful way to check that you have got this aspect of the timing correct is to imagine that each of your

2:1
Ready to punch, shoulders back, hips square

2:2
The punch at halfway stage

2:3
The punch completed

2:4
Tense your muscles
on making contact

hands is grasping the end of a rope which has a pulley at the target area. You can imagine that the left hand has to start the movement by pulling on the rope. This will in turn immediately draw the right fist forward in a straight line directly onto the fulcrum or target.

The movement of the non-attacking hand in providing a balance or compensation for the forward movement of the attack is found in many martial arts techniques. When fully developed it is capable of producing tremendous power in attacks where there isn't much space for manoeuvre. Some experts can perform remarkably powerful punches with as little as 15 centimetres in which to draw their focusing strength.

The compensation factor is not confined just to the arms. The whole body is used to provide as much speed and power as possible by controlled rotation of the hips and shoulders. You see this for yourself as you become more flexible and more experienced in performing the techniques of karate.

Alternating punches
When you feel that you have got the alternating movement correct, you can change your attacking hand. Having completed your right attack you then pull on the 'rope' with your right hand and draw your left fist off the side of your belt and propel it into the target. Remember to turn your left fist so that your thumb is underneath.

When you have completed this left-hand punch and repeated it several times you can

CHAMPION'S TIP

● *When training for punches, ensure that your arms and shoulders are loose. Make a few arm circles at first to relax the shoulder joints. Always begin with slow, easy movements and build up power and speed in stages. Remember to protect your elbow joints by tightening your arm muscles to prevent your elbow suffering 'whiplash' injury.*

begin alternating your attacks. First the right-hand punch, followed by the left, and so on until you have a feeling of relaxed free movement of both arms.

Muscle tensing and arm extension
Now you have got the feeling for the to and fro punching movement, you can try gradual muscle tensing.

Still moving at medium speed, tense the forearm and fist at the point of contact. Don't tense these muscles before impact. Just as you're about to make contact with your imaginary target, turn your fist as explained earlier and tense those muscles. Hold the fist on its target with the muscles tensed for a split second then relax the tension.

Don't begin the alternating punch until you have relaxed tension in the upper arm and fist. If you do so you will quickly get tired.

When you extend your arm to punch the target don't throw the arm out as far as it will go. Doing so will throw a jarring strain on the elbow in a way which the elbow was not designed for. Stop the extension of the arm just before it reaches its locking position against the elbow. Practising in this way will protect the elbow from damage and will avoid the danger of tennis elbow and similar chronic joint trouble in later life.

Increasing the speed
Having mastered the movement and use of the arm muscles, you can now increase the speed of your punching. You will find that, although you can punch a little faster, you're being held back by the non-cooperation of the rest of your body. You must now make use of your whole body.

As you prepare, say, your right fist to deliver its punch, draw back your right hip a little and at the same time pull your right shoulder back very slightly. As you deliver your punch thrust the hip and shoulder forward simultaneously. Do not push either the hip or the shoulder forward beyond the line made by the feet.

The contact of the punch should coincide with the tensing of the hips, shoulders and also the stomach muscles. In addition you should by now be able to control the timing of your muscular reaction. On making contact with your target, you should contract most of the relevant muscles of the body. You can't punch with the hands and arms in isolation, but must call on all parts of the body which can help you in your attempt to punch your opponent. So you also have to tense your buttocks and thighs. At this stage in your training your feet should be firmly on the ground, each of your toes trying to grasp the floor. Your neck should be strong.

Now you can start piling on the speed and the pressure. Remember to keep checking that you are not missing out any steps or making any major mistakes in your techniques. Incorrect techniques learned at this stage will be very difficult to unlearn when you reach the higher stages of karate.

Focus and timing
The last elements in karate punching are what are called focus and timing. Contrary to what some karate instructors teach, it isn't difficult to practise the fundamentals of focus and timing without an actual target to aim at. Nor do you need a body or a punch bag to hit in the early stages. In your mind's

2:5
Press-ups on the backs of your hands – to strengthen your wrists

eye simply choose a target and direct your attack at it.

If you do have access to a punch bag, then by all means use it to perfect your technique. However, there is a danger for beginners who use punch bags. It is very easy to get skinned knuckles. So, as with most karate training, start slowly and carefully. If you want to practise focus and timing by using a punch bag then concentrate just on that. Don't at the same time attempt to use a lot of speed and force.

Another danger in punching too hard is that you may jar or sprain your wrist. Skinned knuckles can take a couple of weeks to repair themselves. An injured wrist has to be rested from impact training of this nature until it has fully recovered, and there is no short cut or other alternative. Time spent recuperating from avoidable injury is time wasted which could better be spent on developing your punching ability.

Fist strengthening for children
Until children are well into their teens, say about 16, their bones are soft and not fully formed. Any youngster doing exercises like knuckle press-ups will run a serious risk of bone damage and malformation of the metacarpals. This damage will be permanent and may also lead to premature arthritis in these joints. It isn't clever or brave for a young teenager to copy older club members whom they see doing such exercises.

They should confine themselves to very short groups of open-handed press-ups and alternate opening and closing of the fingers. This will help in the strong development of their hands and arms without any risk of damage. Children can also practise with

punch bags, remembering not to punch too hard or for too long.

Take care of your wrists
In all punching the part played by the wrists is very important. To complement the job of the fists in punching, the wrists must become both strong and flexible. There is little point in developing a punch which moves like greased lightning if on delivery you suffer a sprained wrist. So from an early stage in punching practice you should also take care to build up your wrists as you increase the strength of your punches.

An exercise for adults
If you're about 18 or over and have been training for two or three months you can try a very useful exercise to strengthen your wrists and increase their flexibility.

Lie face down in the press-up position. Instead of doing open-hand or fist press-ups, do the exercise on the backs of your hands (photo 2:5). At first you will find it hard, a little painful and tiring. Try two or three at first and gradually build up to ten without stopping. It isn't a good idea to perform more than ten, which is enough to exercise the wrist's mobility but not too many to cause any damage.

If you are a complete beginner or a young teenager don't do this exercise, which could cause malformation in the wrist and hands.

Target areas
There are three main target areas, illustrated overleaf, for punches: the head, and particularly the temple (figure 3), the face (figure 4), the chest and stomach area about the waistline (the middle area) (figure 5) and the back (figure 6).

The neck area or anywhere below the waistline are not admissible as scoring areas in competition karate.

No score will be allowed on any part of the arms, on the grounds that they are too well padded with muscle for a punch theoretically to deliver a crippling technique.

The head
Most areas of the head are valid targets for punches and strikes, although they may be limited to certain techniques.

The temple, which is the softest and one of the most vulnerable parts of the head, is a good target for the back fist strike (*uraken*) to score a point (figure 3).

The crown of the head (i.e. the top surface of the head) can be scored on using a

Figures 3-6
The main target areas
for punches:
Figure 3
The temple
Figure 4
The face

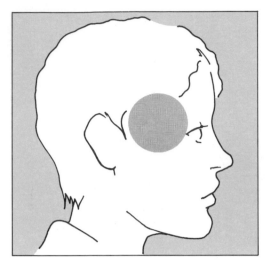

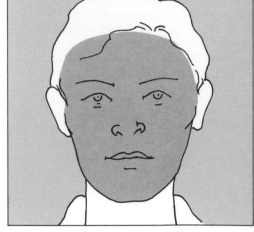

technique called hammer fist (*tet sui*).

Normal punches can score on the face, and also on the back of the head. An attacker who finds and uses the opportunity to punch the back of the head will usually be awarded a full point because someone who is punched in this manner is rarely in a position to do much in the way of defending himself or launching an immediate counter attack.

The face
The face is the most difficult part of the body on which to prove a score. For safety reasons only the lightest touch is allowed. So in competition with both contestants moving around at great speed, it isn't surprising that most punches to the face land short of their goal.

This is particularly true of less experienced karate practitioners, who, in addition to being inexperienced in focusing and judging distance accurately, may have instinctive reservations about risking injury to their sparring partners by punching too far or too hard into the face.

The most dangerous time for face injury is when *karatekas* are developing more confidence with speed and timing. Around this time they tend to go through a phase of hitting their opponents on the face. This may be due to the effect of fine adjustments to their punching range.

Black belts in competition make less face contact than less experienced fighters, partly because they have good defences and also because they have acquired excellent timing and judgement.

Some fighters aim at the forehead, which is the flattest and strongest bone in the head. However, Ticky Donovan, British team

manager since 1982 and world number one karate coach in 1984 and 1986, favours face punches being directed more towards the jaw. The reason is that a defender's natural reaction to a face punch is to throw the head back out of harm's way. But if in so doing the forehead is merely replaced by the nose, a well-judged face punch may become a violent punch on the nose. This could result in a penalty for the attacker and pain for the defender. Throwing the head back to avoid a punch to the chin will reduce this danger.

The middle area
The scoring area on the front of the body stretches from the upper chest down to the area just below the waistline. It also covers most of the ribcage.

The solar plexus area, which is in the top half of the triangle formed by the lower ribs and the waistline, is also a favourite attacking spot. All karate instructors give their students regular exercises to harden the stomach.

The side of the ribs is also a scoring area. Protection of the ribs is usually the responsibility of the arms, which is why it is dangerous to fight with the elbows too far out from the ribcage. As there is little muscle protection around this area, a hard punch can crack or even break a rib or two.

The back
The spine is also a target area from shoulder level down to just below the waistline. As with the back of the head, a person who exposes his unprotected back to his opponent runs a serious risk of being scored on. In a competition you must take care not to let this happen.

There are four occasions when you might

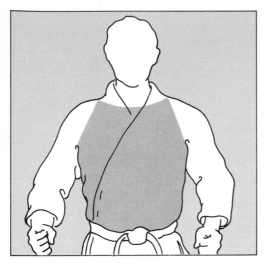

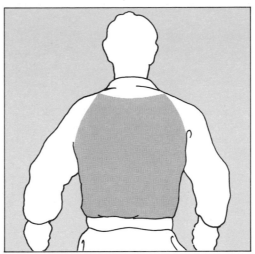

Figure 5
The front middle area
Figure 6
The back

run this risk. The first is if you make a strong attack, especially one where you come rushing forward at your opponent but miss and run past. At that point you must cover yourself by turning to face him again as soon as possible to maintain your protection.

The second is if you think either that you have scored and the referee has called a halt or that the referee has stopped the bout for any reason. You may feel then like relaxing your vigilance. Don't do so unless you are absolutely sure that your opponent has also stopped the proceedings and is returning to his starting mark. Several matches have been lost by a contestant wrongly assuming that the referee had stopped the bout and it was safe to stop and turn away from his opponent, only to receive a punch in the back from his alert and opportunist adversary.

The third example is when you turn your back during the execution of a technique such as a back kick. The fourth example is when, either through superior firepower or demoralization, a contestant feels forced to turn away from his opponent's overwhelming aggression. This kind of action should be avoided by all possible means, since as well as allowing one's opponent free access to the spinal area, the referee may penalize the offender for not taking proper defensive measures.

How hard to punch

Face and head
If you are attacking the facial and head area, you may make only light contact, 'skin touch' as it is often called. If you don't get as close as this your punch will be void and you won't score. If you make very slightly more than light skin contact you will usually

receive a private or informal warning. You will receive a penalty – and your opponent will be awarded a point – if you make reasonably hard contact or you haven't taken enough care with your punch.

If you draw blood, for example inside the lip or cheek or cause a nose bleed, or make excessive contact in the opinion of the referee, you can immediately be disqualified and the bout will be awarded to your opponent.

Body areas
With body punches the standards are different: to score the punch must be delivered with timing and focus. To prove these the punch must make actual contact, delivered with what is called 'controlled force'. That is, it must be a technique potentially powerful enough to put your opponent out of the fight, but the contact must be controlled. In other words you must 'pull' the punch so that it doesn't injure an opponent. So it isn't enough to touch your opponent's target area: you must also land the punch with a mixture of strength and control.

Train to build up muscle and resilience in the target areas of the body, so that at the same time as learning to punch correctly you're becoming stronger and more able to absorb punishment in those parts of the body.

CHAMPION'S TIP

● *When you're in trouble think about the reverse punch. It's the old standby. Don't delay; keep cool and drive it straight in as soon as you see the chance.*

Types of punch

Reverse punch (gyaku zuki)

This is by far the most popular karate attack. It is also the technique which scores more often than any other. There are several reasons for this: it does not require much preparation or body shifting to deliver an effective technique; an expert can build up a lot of speed and power within a relatively short travel; it can often be disguised or concealed by the other hand as it begins its attack and this reduces the time available for the defence; it can also be delivered from practically any position, e.g. moving forward, retreating or just standing still.

It is one of the easier karate punches to perform at basic level. It is, however, a technique which can be, and is, practised and developed by experts to such a degree that it is the favourite and most successful scoring move of great karate champions.

Performing the reverse punch
Face your partner in a left fighting stance with your left leg a comfortable distance in front, knee flexed. The front foot is pointing slightly inwards, never outwards. The rear knee is also slightly bent and the rear foot must point more to the front than to the side. The more your rear foot points sideways the less mobility you will have in your hips. Your feet should be about shoulder width apart sideways, or slightly wider, allowing your hips and shoulder to rest comfortably at an angle of about 45 degrees to your partner.

In this position pull your right hand back to a point beside the top of your right hip where you find it most comfortable. The left hand is out in front as the elbow is bent. The left hand is either open or loosely closed ready for defence or attack (photo 2:6).

From this position drive your right fist forward in a straight line towards the target area, say your partner's chest (photo 2:7). At the same time pull your left hand back in a straight line to rest just above your left hip, ready to follow up with a left-hand attack if necessary (photo 2:8).

Once the punch has been delivered – successfully or not – you should immediately return to a left fighting stance (photo 2:6).

This is the basic movement, but there's more to the punch than this. A technically perfect reverse punch requires full concentration, timing and focus as well as the correct use of the body and its muscles. Simultaneously with the punching movement you begin to push your right hip forward, helping this turn by partially straightening the rear leg. As the punch is going forward push the right shoulder forward also so that it assists the punch to develop maximum power at the moment of impact. The rear foot should remain on the floor. At the moment of contact at least the ball of the foot should be firmly on the ground. All these factors help to make a successful punch.

2:6
Ready for reverse punch

2:7
Reverse punch in flight

2:6

2:7

2:8
Reverse punch
landing: watch your
opponent, not your
fist

2:9
Reverse punch: take
care not to over-reach

2:10
Moving reverse punch:
keep the elbows down

Finding more distance
The turning movement of the hips, together
with the push of the shoulder, will help
greatly towards both obtaining more power
and gaining distance. When you start
practising this technique you will find that
you can't reach very far with it. This is
because you are probably not rotating your
hip and pushing forward with your rear leg.
As your body becomes more flexible and
your hips less stiff you'll find that the range
of your reverse punch is gradually increasing
and eventually that you can make a strong
punch onto a more distant target.

Posture and balance
There is so much to remember when first
learning how to punch that posture is
sometimes ignored. The way in which you
hold your body in reverse punching can be
vital to the success of your punch.

As you build up the movement of this
punch and your hips move round more
freely, you will reach a point at which you
feel physically comfortable delivering a

punch. Then you should stop and set your
limit.

If you turn your hips too much you may
risk injuring your lower back, causing joint
pain on making the turning movement and a
pain like groin strain, which is not a
hamstring injury but 'referred pain' from the
lower back strain.

A second result of over-reaching in your
technique will be that you become over-
balanced, usually to the front. This means
that your punch will have passed the point at
which it was an effective technique and it
will be burnt out. In addition, your whole
body, being off balance will be temporarily
not under your full control. Your opponent
will be able to attack you while you are
struggling to regain your balance, composure and attacking stance (photo 2:9).

A useful way to help maintain your
posture is to remember that the position of
the head will determine the angle of the
body. If you keep your head up and look
straight ahead you will preserve your
balance. If you look down onto the floor or

let your head swing from side to side as you punch, you will lose direction and force.

Advancing reverse punch

To use a reverse punch on an opponent who is either out of range or moving backwards – which is often the case in combat – you have to move forward to deliver your punch.

If you start in left fighting stance, you step forward with your right foot (photo 2:10). As you begin your step you must quickly reverse the position of your hands. Your arms must move speedily enough so that before you have finished the step forward your left hand has pulled back and is in a position to make a left reverse punch into your opponent. Speed with the hands is also important because during the change of position your front area must be unprotected for as short a time as possible (photo 2:11).

On moving forward move the rear foot in a semi-circular motion, almost brushing the insides of both ankles as you come forward. This is to protect your groin area as you make your attacking move.

Retreating reverse punch

This punch can also be applied effectively while you are stepping backwards. The same principles apply to a punch delivered from this position. The main difference is the sudden push put on the rear leg which stops your rearward movement, followed by thrusting forward to assist the punch. It can surprise someone who thinks he has the advantage and is pushing his opponent backwards to the edge of the fighting area.

Someone walking forward in attack is more vulnerable to an attack from underneath than to one from middle or upper level (photo 2:16, overleaf).

There are two punches which are delivered with the front hand, the lunge punch (*oi zuki*) and the snap punch (*kizami zuki*). Punches by the leading hand may not be as powerful as those by the rear hand as they have only a short distance to gather momentum and force, so they need other qualities to make them effective scoring techniques.

2:11
Advancing reverse punch: stretch forward keeping your head upright

2:12

Lunge punch (*oi zuki*)

This powerful punch starts its life in the fist of the rear hand. From left fighting stance tighten the hips and quickly move forward, using the semi-circular step, as explained earlier. As you are nearing the end of your step drive the right arm forward in a straight line into the target. If you are aiming for the chest, keep your body upright and your head erect. Try to coincide the end of your step with the arrival on target of your punch, which you twist into position. In this way you maximize the effect of the arm movement and the step forward (photo 2:13 and 2:14).

As with all punches, the more muscle you use in the right way and at the right time, the more positive will be your punch. As you complete the move tighten your stomach and shoulder muscles, relaxing them immediately your punch has landed.

2:13

Opportunities for the lunge punch

This is a very powerful punch. An uncontrolled lunge punch might cause serious injury, such as broken ribs or internal damage.

To build up the power needed for this attack you must use the body's weight and forward momentum as much as possible. As this punch requires so much forward movement, there is little point in using it if you are close to your opponent. If you find yourself a couple of steps away from him during a bout he may well relax for a split second, not expecting any immediate attack. This is a good opportunity to come rushing in with such a punch. If you are quick enough, he may not have got his arm defences in position properly by the time he realizes what you have in mind and the power of your thrust could drive through them and score on his chest.

The lunge punch to the face and head area (*oi zuki jodan*) is a favourite technique of the Japanese. Their top fighters can dart in from great distances and plant a lunge punch right on the tip of their opponents' noses with incredible speed, demonstrating a very high degree of control. A lunge punch to the head area requires a firmly planted rear foot to give stability and thrust up through the body and shoulder to the fist (photo 2:14).

2:15
Lunge punch to face; force your way through your opponent's guard

2:16
Lunge punch: contact. Use your rear leg for extra power

2:14

2:12
Lunge punch: front view; make yourself as small a target as possible

2:13
Lunge punch; keep your opponent at a distance as you move in

2:14
Lunge punch: although your opponent is retreating, your attack is strong

2:17

Hammer fist (*tet sui*)

The use of this technique in competition is comparatively rare, but it has occasionally been used successfully in major championships.

You are both in left fighting stance. You suddenly spring up in the air and bring your right fist over to thump your opponent on the top of his head with the underside (little finger edge) of your fist. Your left hand should be used to block any attack from your opponent and you can also use it to gain some extra height at your opponent's expense, if possible.

It's a technique which lends itself to lighter and more agile performers. Photos 2:17 to 2:19 show a typical hammer fist attack in action

2:17
Hammer fist; jump up at your opponent's side

2:18
Hammer fist: control the defender's right hand as you go up

2:19
Hammer fist: a clean, controlled attack to the crown of your opponent's head

2:20
Snap punch to face: don't give your opponent any warning

2:21
Snap punch aimed at the chin, thumb uppermost

Front snap punch (*kizami zuki*)

This punch is a fast technique which relies more on its surprise value than the power of its delivery. It is performed by the front hand and the target can be your opponent's face. The difference between it and the lunge punch is that with the snap punch you don't change stance: it comes suddenly from your leading hand with no other obvious preparatory moves being made.

You and your opponent are in left fighting stance. Your left hand moves forward to punch your opponent in the facial area. In this technique your fist doesn't turn at all, but moves in a straight line to the face and makes its contact with the thumbside uppermost, little finger end pointing downwards.

As this punch travels a shorter distance, it's more difficult to get enough speed and power behind it to make it into a good scoring technique. This takes practice, which you can do with a partner or, as many *karateka* do, by yourself. If training by yourself look, for example, at a point on the wall and try to judge the distance accurately before you start building up the speed. Once you have mastered just how far to drive your punch, you can start building up a fast technique.

When training with a partner make sure that he stands quite still with his hands in the normal fighting position (photo 2:20). The left hand goes straight forward towards your opponent's face. It is better to aim at the chin (photo 2.21) so that if he throws his head back you are unlikely to injure him on any other part of his face. The photographs below show the effect of a snap punch to the nose which the defender tried to avoid by lifting his head up and out of harm's way! Photos 2.22 and 2.23 show the danger of a misjudged snap punch.

2:20

2:21

2:22
Snap punch to nose:
defender's head
automatically goes
back

2:23
Snap punch: head
thrown back means
penalty for contact
with the jaw

Back fist strike (*uraken*)

This technique is popular and easy to perform at a basic level. However, to score in competition it has to be delivered with great speed and precision. It is delivered with the back of the fist in a snapping movement onto the target, which may be the head. Photo 2:24 shows the attacker's forward stance at the start of a back fist strike.

To produce the sudden whip-lash power required for this strike, bring your front hand back towards your jaw. Your elbow must also come up to provide the necessary leverage at the correct angle (photo 2:25). From this position the arm must spring out and the back of the fist must make skin contact only with the target (photo 2:26). Raise the arm to reach over the opponent's defending arms.

To achieve the sudden unleashing of the fist in this technique, twist the whole body a little to allow for the full movement of the attack. The rear hand also pulls strongly back at the same time.

2:24
Before back fist strike: elbow forward, fist pulled back

CHAMPION'S TIPS

● *Practise in front of a mirror and send out the fist horizontally*

● *Hold the fist up in the referee's line of vision*

● *On completion bring the fist back immediately to protect your front*

2:25
Back fist strike: score by striking over your opponent's guard

As a contrast to the speed with which the back fist must be used it must also stop on the target for a split second to prove that it's on target and that sufficient control has been used in its execution. A strike can be fast and precise, but unless the referee can see that it is on target and performed with control, it won't score.

A technique which lands on the ear, neck or cheek won't score. The reason for the precise scoring requirement is that although this is an extremely fast attack, there is not much power behind it: it's likely to do real damage only to a particularly vulnerable area, like the temple, rather than the bony protuberance of the cheek or the resilience of a well-developed well-muscled neck area.

When to use the back fist strike

The advice on when to use the back fist strike is 'sparingly'. It tends to be over-used, particularly among beginners, because of the apparent ease with which it can be done and also because it can look impressive and dangerous to beginners and to those who know little about karate. Someone who uses a lot of back fist strikes won't be very successful as it will soon become known among his opponents, who will have little trouble anticipating and spoiling his attacks.

When you use a back fist strike mix with it other techniques, particularly middle area punches. If your opponent has got his mind on defending his chest area he'll be less able to counter your sudden back fist strike coming at him over the top of his front arm.

2:26
Close up of back fist score

Beware retaliation

As you can see from photo 2:25, a back fist requires you to reach out over your opponent's guard. You will also see that it isn't too difficult for him to bring up his front hand a little to block your attack (photo 2:27). At that moment you are open to attack: you have stretched out, your body is turned slightly out, your right hand is too far away to be of any use and your left chest area is only a short distance away from his right fist.

Once your opponent has put his left-hand blocking procedure into operation, he can concentrate on retaliatory measures in the form of a counter punch into your chest. This is what is happening in photo 2:29.

If you perform a back fist strike which is successful and it is followed by a counter attack, say a reverse punch to your body, you will be awarded the point because you were the first to score. However, if you miss with your strike, or it is not performed effectively, and your opponent – whether he blocks it or not – puts in a good counter attack he will be awarded the point on the grounds that you attempted a scoring technique and failed whereas he attempted and succeeded.

In spite of the few drawbacks to the back fist strike, it is a very useful technique and properly used scores many points at all levels of competition.

2:27
During a back fist strike your opponent could block with his hand . . .

2:28
. . . open up your left chest area . . .

2:29
. . . and score with a punch under your outstretched arm

POWER DRILL

★ When practising your back fist strike the hip twist is important

★ Tight hips will slow you down and restrict their pivoting movement

★ Lift your body and arm enough to clear your opponent's defence, but not so high that he is able to counter you underneath your own attack

---

POWER DRILL

★ *Improve your backfist strikes by mirror training. Simultaneously drive out your fist and twist your hips the opposite way. The two movements should coincide and finish their action at the same time. Practise with both fists. Keep the fists closed and strong, but not too tight.*

KICKS

Kicking in karate is different from any other form of kicking which you may have done. Karate kicks begin with the leg bent at the knee; the leg is then straightened to hit the target with the foot as the initial swing is reaching its maximum power at the end of its driving movement. This principle is common to all the major kicks in karate.

Kicks are slower and need more preparation than punches, but they are stronger and have a longer reach than punches.

The target areas
These are the chest area to the waistline (photo 3:1), i.e. the belt; the side of the head (photo 3:2), also the front of the head i.e. the face area, also the back of the head with certain kicks; the tops of the shoulders; side of the chest wall (photo 3:3, overleaf), and the back of the body, above the hips; the spine area from shoulder to waistline.

3:1
Front kick: a score to the chest

3:2
Scoring a point with a head kick. The foot has cleared the shoulder and made direct contact with the side of the head

Opposite: Power and concentration are clearly visible in this head kick

3:3
Front kick into rib
cage. Don't come in
too close

3:4
Front kick: keep your
upper body clear of
your opponent's
punching range

A kick aimed at a scoring area but which misses and hits, for example, the upper arm, won't score. A kick to the groin won't score and may be penalized (photo 3:5). Except for viable footsweeps, kicks to the legs and knee joints are absolutely forbidden and flagrant disregard of this rule will bring disqualification from the match.

Use of the knee

To develop a strong and flowing kicking movement you should begin by standing in normal fighting stance (photo 2:6, page 20). Practise lifting the rear leg forward, knee first, as if to deliver a knee attack (photo 3:6, overleaf). Keep the front foot stationary and the arms in the fighting position. Bring the knee forward and upwards to waist height and then drop it back down.

Repeat this movement ten times. Reverse your stance and do this exercise ten times with the other leg.

Opening out the hips

It's very important to combine this practice with hip flexibility exercises. Tight hips will restrict your movement.

You can exercise your hips by doing some of the movements shown in photos 3:8 and 3:9, overleaf. You mustn't put strain on your joints or ligaments by doing excessive or 'bouncing' exercises which can result in permanent damage to your limbs in later life.

In addition flexibility must go together with strength. If you make your hip joints more flexible you must also do muscle-building exercises so that your joints are held together by equally well-developed muscles.

Keeping your balance

It's not much use putting an attractive looking kick into your opponent if in so doing you lose control of your own balance.

There's a tendency when performing

3:5
Foul!

kicks – and especially roundhouse attacks – to wave the arms about or stick them out to the sides. This is a natural means of retaining balance, but one which you must avoid. If you begin karate competition by waving your arms about when kicking you'll find it difficult to break the habit later.

Successful fighting karate depends on many factors and one of the more important ones is not to telegraph to your opponent what you are going to do. Arms suddenly going out to the side is a sure sign that a kick is on the way.

Several of the action photographs in this book show fighters performing kicks with their hands outstretched and their guard apparently ineffective. Top competitors are so fast and so experienced that they can afford to take such chances. You'll see for example how they lean away from their opponents as they make their attacks. All their concentration is on making contact with their kicks. Before reaching that stage of competence you must master the basics of technique and balance.

To test your balance try standing on one leg. Try both sides. Do the same thing while balancing on the ball of the supporting foot. Finally, try kicking into the air while hopping about on the supporting leg. You will find it difficult and tiring at first since this exercise makes the lower limb muscles work very hard. So practise gently at first and gradually increase the power and scope of the practice.

Another exercise is to swing your straight leg forwards and backwards as far and as high as you can without straining your hips or groin. Lean your body forwards as necessary to increase the range of your backwards swing. As with all such exercises, easy practice at first will increase your balance. Trying too hard may cause strain or even injury which will hold back your progress as you spend time recovering.

You might also try swinging your legs to the left and the right sideways across the front of your body. As with the other exercise, train within your own flexibility and safety limits.

In karate training, especially while you are still inexperienced, you should never cross your legs even briefly. By doing so you make yourself into a prime target for a foot sweep. When moving around keep your balance by maintaining a sideways separation of your feet, say the width of your own shoulders, as well as a lengthwise gap.

3:6
Knee up for front kick, strong but flexible

3:7
Front kick showing
tension in the muscles

3:8
Flexibility training for
roundhouse kick.

3:9
Roundhouse kick:
raising and turning
hips on the move

:8

3:9

POWER DRILL

★ *When training for kick attacks all your muscles are important, but a tensed foot is the key to scoring. As you contract your muscles for connection you must also push out. Don't allow muscle contraction to frustrate your kick.*

❛ If you turn sideways on towards your opponent, confuse him by feinting with your front foot, but then switch to an attack with your rear leg. Cover yourself against his counter.❜

In position for kicking

There is a tendency in combat to turn 90 degrees sideways to your opponent, which feels safer because not such a broad target is presented to the opponent. However, this is false logic and disadvantageous for two reasons: standing in this position leaves your back area open to attack, usually with a roundhouse kick or a foot sweep; it also severely restricts your own ability to attack your opponent – and he will know that. Nor can you bring up your rear fist or foot to deliver a speedy attack.

The ideal stance to take up when beginning combat is to face your opponent at an angle of between 30 and 45 degrees from the front. This is the best compromise between the ideal attacking position and being a difficult target for your opponent.

Put out your leading foot and point it either directly ahead or preferably slightly inwards. Don't ever point it outwards, as this affects the body's co-ordination and ability to deliver techniques properly. Your rear foot should be pointing mostly to the front, never out to the side. If it points sideways you will soon find that you can't bring the hip round and tense your body's muscles for the big punch that you wish to put into your opponent (photo 3:10). Your feet should be about shoulder width apart.

Your knees should be slightly bent, with the upper and lower leg muscles relaxed but ready for instant action, prepared to move forward into attack or sideways or backwards in defence.

Your body should be upright, as this gives the greatest range of movement for whatever move you decide to make, or are forced to make. If you receive a hard body punch try never to fold up or bend your body forward in trying to avoid the blow. With a bent trunk it's difficult to harden your stomach muscles and if you're weak in that area you're likely to be winded by a well-delivered technique. Pluck up the courage to show a strong fearless front to your opponent. It will impress him and protect you.

Finally, don't wave your arms around. Keep your head steady and watch your opponent all the time. This will stop you becoming disoriented and losing track of your position. At first the arms can be kept close to the body with the elbows down to protect the ribcage, although with experience you will soon be able to judge when you can put your hands out towards your opponent, both to distract him and to foil his intended attack.

Using the knee

The kneecap (patella) is one of the hardest bones in the body. Drawing up the knee and shin can be very useful as an emergency defence if you suspect a kick or other middle area attack is about to be launched against you. The knee can also be used as an attack in itself, although it's not used in sport karate competition for safety reasons. To deliver a knee attack you should point the foot down towards the floor. This tightens the muscles and ligaments and assists the knee thrust. Note that this is different from the foot position in beginning the front kick, where

the foot and toes are pulled back to produce the hard pad on the ball of the foot. If you have to use a knee strike you'll have more chance of success against your attacker's stomach or lower chest area than against the more popular, but less accessible, groin area.

Positioning of the knees and legs can help to confuse your opponent. Constant change of the position of your knees and legs and occasional feinting with your knee raised can be useful in unsettling your opponent. Note: If he starts watching your legs, come in with a middle area punch.

3:10
Kicking position: with the rear foot pointing sideways your hips can't be brought into the attacking position

3:11
Kicking position: by standing sideways the fighter on the right has left himself defenceless against his opponent's foot sweep

3:12
Front kick: the raised knee helps to protect you

3:13
Front kick: the ball of your foot is the weapon

3:14
Front kick: maintain cover also with your arms

Types of kick

Front kick (*mae geri*)

In this kick you face your opponent in the fighting stance. The front foot remains stationary, front knee slightly bent. Remember that the rear foot should be pointing more to the front than to the side. Bring up the rear leg, knee first as if to deliver a knee attack (photo 3:12). Keep the body upright, push the hips forward and straighten the knee as you come to the climax of your forward movement. With toes curled back thrust the ball of the foot into the target area (usually your opponent's stomach or chin, photo 3:14).

On completion of the attack retract your attacking foot at once by bending your knee and only then dropping your leg to the floor (photo 3:15). Whether your step is to the front or to the rear depends on whether you want to pursue your advantage with a follow-up attack or defend and/or move out of the way of your opponent's counter attack. Withdrawing your leg immediately helps to maintain your balance and also quickly returns you to a position where you can pursue another attack.

The front kick is one of the most powerful techniques.

Foot position

The position of the foot and toes is vital to gain the point. The foot is taut, toes curled

---

CHAMPION'S TIPS

● *Don't fully straighten your leg when starting to practise this technique. You will avoid damage to your knee joint and improve your balance*

● *Don't telegraph your intention to kick by lifting up your body just before beginning the attack*

● *Nor should you wave your arms about before the kick*

3:16
Front kick: try to keep your toes out of harm's way

3:15
Front kick: speedy recovery after delivery, protecting yourself all the time

right back (close-up photo 3:13, page 42). Straight toes can get caught in your opponent's karate suit and be dislocated or broken (photo 3:16).

Practise this move with a partner. Step forward with your kick aimed at your partner's middle. Your partner steps back and returns the kick, this time with you skipping back. Both stay in the same stances and keeping the stances for your skips back.

Then change to your opponent attacking first, you retreating and then skipping forward with a reciprocal attack on your rear foot.

After each has had ten kicks as attacker and defender, change your stances and attack each other as above but with the other foot.

Roundhouse kick (*mawashi geri*)

This is a very effective and spectacular technique. It is more difficult than a front kick, but it is worth the extra practice and effort to produce a good one. The object is to kick round your opponent's guard, which he normally holds up in front of him facing you, and deliver a blow to the side, or rear side of his body or to the side of his head.

Success with the roundhouse kick requires good hip flexibility and you should try the hip-opening exercises described earlier in this chapter. The first requirement is to bring the knee up and to the side rather than straight in front as in the front kick (photo 3:17). This is difficult but becomes easier with practice. From the outside bring the bent knee round to the front, at the same time straightening your knee. The final push round of your leg and the straightening of the knee should combine to produce a powerful strike onto the target area (photo 3:18). As with the front kick don't fully straighten the knee in the early stages to avoid damaging the knee joint.

Roundhouse kick to the middle area

At first you should aim only for the middle area of the body, that is above the belt and below the shoulders. If you kick your opponent on the hip it won't score and you will also hurt yourself more than you hurt him. Similarly, a kick into the shoulder which is well padded with muscle won't score and may hurt you more than your opponent. Get your distance right. The roundhouse kick is not a technique for close combat and needs more room than a front kick.

When you are more proficient you can try bringing your knee up to the front more, as in the front kick, and suddenly turning to a roundhouse. This move will make your opponent undecided as to whether a front or a roundhouse kick is coming. If his arms are still defending against what he expected to be a front kick, his side will be exposed and will be easier to score on. In addition, your knee up high in front of you will impede any counter attack he may try to make.

Roundhouse kick to the head

The other target area for the roundhouse kick is the head, usually the side area. It is absolutely vital that this kick is controlled and beginners shouldn't attempt it. It requires a high degree of timing, focus and strength to control, as well as great leg and hip flexibility to reach the required height (photo 3:19).

Roundhouse kick:
3:17
Raise the knee before beginning to swing the leg round

3:18
Reach well round and into the target

3:17

3:18

Practising this kick at middle area height will improve the qualities necessary to deliver it properly. With this practice you will gradually be able to deliver one of karate's most powerful and spectacular techniques. Keep your leading hand in front of you to block or deflect any counter attack your opponent may make when he knows or suspects that a roundhouse kick is on its way.

The danger with this kick is that too much force on the side of the head may cause concussion or temporary unconsciousness. Someone falling down as the result of such damage may land heavily and badly and even fracture his skull. So it is important when practising this technique to use the minimum of force. If you ever suspect that your partner is groggy or unsteady when you are training with him, stop immediately and inform your instructor. Similarly, if you feel dizzy or unstable you must stop and let your instructor know.

As with all karate techniques, a roundhouse kick has to be on target to score. A middle area kick won't score if it's partially blocked by your opponent's arm. If the point of his elbow catches your foot it will also hurt you! Your opponent's defending arm has to be negotiated to score with this kick. To achieve this you should aim to plant the top surface of your foot onto his back area rather than being satisfied with merely striking the side of his body.

CHAMPION'S TIPS

● *Don't shuffle about or keep looking at the target*

● *When kicking keep your body taut and compact*

● *Try to start the kick out of your opponent's range of vision*

3:19
Roundhouse kick: note the attacker's good balance in this head attack

★ *For reverse roundhouse kick practice you should pull your knee up tightly against your chest, toes pointing down. Pull tight and then relax. Do this five times with each leg. Then repeat the exercise on each leg, but this time pulling the knee left and right across your front to stretch the ligaments.*

Reverse roundhouse kick:
3:20
You must start well balanced with your knee raised high

3:21
Make a scything movement up as far as the side of your opponent's head

3:22
Twist your hip and upper body as you swing your leg up his body

3:23
Cover yourself on completion and land safely

Reverse roundhouse kick (*gyaku mawashi geri*)

This spectacular technique often scores a full point when performed well against an opponent's head. It is a difficult kick for the beginner to master, because it requires a lot of hip flexibility as well as good timing and muscle control.

Both of you are facing up in left front stance. You bring up your right leg, bent at the knee. Raise the knee high and twist the body to the left. As you turn your body in a tight circle, extend your right leg so that it goes out and up to your opponent's right front. You then start to bend your leg at the knee in a scything motion to catch the side of your opponent's head with your foot. Don't use your heel, but try to place the sole of your foot as much as possible against the side of your opponent's head.

You must be very careful not to use a full-force kick when performing this technique. The movement to aim for is a 'placing' one, as if you want to touch the sole of the foot against the side of the head and then bring it back down again with as much muscle control as possible (photos 3:20, 3:21 and 3:22).

As you will have gathered, this kick must be practised very carefully. As well as being penalized for using excessive force, you may also give your opponent a head injury through your carelessness or over-ambitious use of this technique. It is a good idea to start learning this kick by performing it at chest level. In this way you can develop the basic twisting and reverse kicking motion first. Then follow it by aiming higher up the body

3:20

3:21

3:22

3:23

until you have the control and focus to place the sole of your foot against the side of your opponent's head.

To withdraw after performing the kick you must pull the foot back and away from its target and bring the leg back roughly along the same line as it went up to its target. You should place the foot back on the floor cleanly and well on balance (photo 3:23).

Until you're proficient at this kick don't 'follow through', as you may injure your opponent with your foot which is by now flying at high speed through the air. In addition, if your opponent has evaded your kick or it has missed, you will be off balance and open as you land and he will be able to choose his moment and place on which to score on you (photo 3:24).

Recovery from the roundhouse kick
It is important to maintain your balance at all times during training and in competition. Coming back to a stable stance as soon as possible is your priority after performing a roundhouse kick.

Once you have delivered your kick, whether it has scored or not, you must bend the knee of your attacking leg and bring the leg back to the ground in a controlled manner as soon as possible. You must land in a strong and stable stance. Don't let your feet fall into a straight line, because in this position you are ripe for a counter attack – probably a tripping technique – from your opponent. Landing in a strong stance gives you the ability to go immediately into the attack again with whatever technique you like.

❝ The ideal reverse roundhouse is not seen by the victim. Its twisting movement is deceptive and its flight is difficult to follow.❞

3:24
Reverse roundhouse kick: a bad landing is dangerous

CHAMPION'S TIP

● *Always bring your knee up quite high before thrusting out your side kick. You invariably tend to lose height in this kick, so begin it with plenty of initial lift.*

Side kick (*yoko geri*)

The force of this kick goes out sideways from the body rather than forwards. It is difficult and requires considerable hip flexibility to perform correctly.

The side kick, although an effective technique in isolation, is less frequently seen in competitive karate matches because it usually takes a little longer to complete than other kicks. Nevertheless it is well worth while perfecting and those top fighters who do favour it can perform the side kick with devastating effect.

From freestyle stance bring up the rear leg, bent at the knee. Raise this knee quite high, at least to waist height. At the same time turn the body to a right-angled (90-degree) position away from your opponent, making sure that your raised knee and both arms are covering your body against a counter attack (photo 3:25). Now drive your leg straight out sideways from your hip, in a straight line attack towards the target (photo 3:26). Note that the part of the foot which strikes the target is the outside edge, or on occasion the heel can be used. Make sure that your foot goes out straight and doesn't drop and kick your opponent below the belt.

It is important to bring the foreleg back quickly by bending the knee again immediately after delivering this attack. Leaving the leg stretched out in the side kick position leaves the attacker open to a variety of counter moves.

Remember also that, although the kick is delivered in a sideways movement away from the body, the head should always face the opponent so that he can be kept constantly in view.

Side kick variation

A useful variation of the side kick is the front foot side kick. This is delivered by kicking from the front foot, just turning the body slightly to the side opposite the leg that is performing the technique. Remember to

3:25
Side kick: raise the knee high for protection as well as reach

cover the body with the hands during this kick. To perform it quickly and with power, it's important not to begin in a deep stance. An upright and high stance will allow you to lift the leg quickly and maintain your balance as you thrust the kick home into the target.

Do remember that with this technique you are at your most vulnerable when you have delivered the kick and are withdrawing your leg before replacing it on the floor. At that moment you are generally not fully balanced and so may not be able to defend yourself against your opponent's counter attack. An experienced opponent will know when to put in his counter, which is when you are putting your foot back down and recovering your balance. So it is necessary either to cover yourself efficiently after your technique or else to follow the kick with another technique which will make your opponent protect himself further instead of trying to take advantage of your momentarily reduced defences.

The most common use of the front foot side kick is as a counter itself. It is useful where, for example, your opponent comes rushing in straight towards you in the hope of forcing you backwards and driving a punch or two into you. If you can anticipate such an attack you can raise your front leg and force it straight into his chest or stomach area.

The combined force of your side thrust meeting his forward rush in his chest area can not only score a good point, but may also wind him and adversely affect him during the rest of the bout or until he gets his wind back.

In using the side kick in this manner make sure that your supporting leg is firmly in contact with the floor and you're braced for the jolt which this violent connection can make. As soon as you've delivered the technique withdraw your foot by bending the knee again and dropping the foot to the floor in a controlled manner.

3:26
Side kick: stretch out the leg with focus and power

3:27
Start of a back kick:
keep your opponent at
bay while you turn

3:28
A good back kick,
which has forced the
opponent to bend in
the middle

Back kick (*ushiro geri*)

Generally speaking you should never turn your back on your opponent, either accidentally or in an effort to escape attack. However, occasionally you may find yourself in that position or nearly in that position and you have an opportunity to attack. Clearly it will take too long to turn round and attack with any of the techniques so far described. The answer may well be to use the back kick, in which the foot is driven out to the rear and directly into your opponent's body.

Practise this technique first by standing with your back to your partner. Step back with your front foot to a point beside your rear foot still facing away from your partner. Now lift your rear knee up towards your front. Swing your leg back and drive it out parallel to the floor. Keep the foot pointing down if you can and drive the heel into your opponent's stomach or chest.

Try this several times and then attempt the same technique by starting off turns at 90 degrees from your opponent. Swing your body round and turn so that you can deliver a back kick straight towards your opponent. You will find that this may make you a little dizzy if you do it too many times, so just try it as often as you can comfortably manage.

With more practice you can try facing your partner and turning your body through 180 degrees to deliver a back kick into his midriff. In detail, for example, stand in left free fight stance facing your partner with the left foot in front. Turn your whole body fully round to your right until you are facing completely away from him. As you turn start to raise your right (rear) knee. As you finish turning your body thrust your right foot backwards into your partner's middle. This is a difficult move and you should start from the basic backward position and only gradually build up to the full body turn and kick (photos 3:27 and 3:28).

When delivering this kick you should lean away from your opponent. This will both give your kick more momentum and power from the pivoting effect of your hips and the rest of your body, and move your upper body away and out of reach of any counter he may try to put in your direction.

Always turn your head and look over your shoulder at your target. It's impossible to score a hit with this technique unless you are guiding it in towards your opponent. By watching its progress you can make those split-second alterations in direction to compensate for your opponent's defensive moves.

On completing this technique always land facing your opponent again, so that you're ready for the next attack, whether from yourself or from your opponent.

Flexibility and power

A person who knows how to use his legs properly has a tremendous advantage in karate. The correct and effective use of legs doesn't just include flexibility. Some people are fortunate enough to have very loose joints in their lower limbs; high kicks and leg splits, for example, seem to come naturally to them. But flexibility itself will not score points.

A very high kick may look impressive but it's worthless unless it's accompanied by power, that is the muscle development and control to drive home the attack.

People with naturally flexible legs often don't have the power to make them into effective kicks. With most other people the reverse is true: the leg muscles are so well developed that they constantly resist attempts to extend the joints and ligaments. So naturally flexible people have to build up muscle for power, whereas those with more muscular and stiffer legs need to attain flexibility by gradually stretching and loosening their limbs.

Controlled aggression

Targeting and focus are more difficult in kicking than in punching. You have much more awareness of your armreach than of the range of your legs. Your kicks, therefore, need more practice in this area.

The vast majority of newer *karateka* carefully and gradually mould their technique from a distance until they can kick strongly, but with control, to make light contact. A very few people appear unable to take this line and go in on full power with every kick. This is very disconcerting for their partners and it's bad karate. True controlled aggression is being able to perform a powerful technique, but with self-control and physical restraint in pulling back the kick at the moment of contact so that your partner is not injured.

BLOCKING ATTACKS

*All basic moves in karate begin with a block which precedes the main attacking technique. The reason for this is to remind the *karateka* that the true spirit of karate is never to initiate aggression but to defend first and attack second.*

In any combat sport you have to learn how to defend yourself against your opponent. It is no good developing good attacking moves if they aren't accompanied by the study of defensive techniques. There are some extremely good attacking fighters who, because they haven't mastered the art of competent defence, don't, and won't ever, make it to the top.

Let's examine in detail what happens in a fight. You're doing two separate, but related, things. First you're looking for ways of scoring on your opponent; that's uppermost in your mind. But at the same time you're also watching him because you know that he's doing exactly the same thing to you. If your opponent decides to attack it's a matter of luck as to how much warning you'll receive of his intention to send a fist or a foot flying through the air in the direction of your body. The decisions that are made by him, but even more so those made by you, now happen within a very short, almost immeasurable, space of time. If you're lucky or if, say, your opponent is relatively inexperienced, you may get a warning of some kind, or even sense that he's about to attack. These warning signs and tactical manoeuvres are discussed in more detail in the chapter on karate competitions.

For the present let's say that your opponent has decided to attack you. Your immediate perception of the attack is passed to your brain, which then sends a message telling you to avoid the technique. If you haven't yet identified what kind of attack is being made the message from your brain can only be a general defensive one and will be accompanied by a request for more information: for example, is it a kick or a punch?

Once your brain has been informed that an attack is genuinely or probably under way your brain will seek more information so that it can send the appropriate instructions to the body for defensive action to be used. The information which the brain will seek will be, for example: Is the attack a kick or a punch, or some other move? At what area of my body is it being directed? Is the attack likely to succeed: for example, is my attacker perhaps too far away to reach me? What are my defences like in the area he is attacking?

Do I need to reinforce my protection there?

These questions and many other related ones have to be answered within a split second and the appropriate defensive action prepared and executed. Often what looks initially like a threatened attack will collapse into a non-event, perhaps because you realize that your opponent is too far away to reach you or he himself doesn't follow through with it. In these circumstances your brain, on being told that the attack is no longer under way, will tell the body's defences to stand down until the next alert is received.

However, if the alert is justified by a purposeful and potentially successful attack, you have to decide on the most effective way of stopping the attack reaching home. The best way to ensure that your opponent's punch or kick doesn't reach its target is for you not to be around when his technique reaches its goal. In combat the initiative lies with the person making the attack. It is instinctive for the person being attacked to try to jump clear of any danger and this method is the most commonly used way of avoiding a threat.

However, it's impractical and counterproductive merely to keep moving your body position away from attacks. If you do your opponent will quickly find a way of scoring on you. Also a constantly retreating fighter will find great difficulty in producing kicks and punches sufficiently powerful to score on an advancing opponent. The answer to this problem is that you have to block your opponent's attacks using the other means at your disposal, that is your arms, hands and your body if necessary.

Blocking attacks to the head

There are two main methods of blocking or deflecting punches or kicks to your head, an upper rising block (*jodan age uke*) and outside arm block (*soto ude uke*). The open-hand block is used against kicks to the head.

Upper rising block (*jodan age uke*)
When you feel that the punch is about to be delivered to your head move your leading hand from a threatening on-guard position

Opposite: After blocking an attack the defender has already begun to step in with her counter

POWER DRILL

★ *To make a strong block punch the hand up in front of you as if to deliver an uppercut. As the block passes your face turn your fist out and up into a powerful deflection.*

back and up to a deflecting block position. The movement is a tensing of the forearm and a twisting out of the fist, so that the underside of the clenched fist faces your opponent. Keep the elbow lower than the hand and make contact with your attacker's wrist area from underneath his arm, deflecting it up and to the side away from your head (photo 4:1).

As with all karate blocks, when done well and with power, this block will help upset your opponent's balance and will also force him into a position in which he is open to a counter attack from you.

Outside arm block (*soto ude uke*)

In this defensive move your opponent is attacking your head with a right-hand punch to the head. Your front hand, e.g. your left, opens out and drives the attacking punch sideways to your right across your frontal area.

The particular advantage of this block is that it both deflects your opponent's punch and turns his whole body round and away from you.

This greatly reduces the chance of his being able to change to a left-hand attack, since he will find it too difficult to bring his left fist round the front of his body and deliver a punch. Moreover, a good performance in this blocking technique will position you ideally for a strong counter attack against an opponent whose defences you have just destroyed.

Stopping a back fist strike

The back fist strike (*uraken*) is the fastest technique used in competition karate. However, it isn't very powerful and the target area is restricted to the side of the head around the temple.

The back fist strike is usually delivered by the front fist, so in general you should watch the front hand for signs of an impending attack. While it is impossible to read your opponent's mind, you may find some clues in his stances. A person about to try this surprise attack often stands up a bit straighter just before his move. This is an unconscious movement and is designed to give more reach over your defending arms. When you suspect this you must be more vigilant and try to anticipate if and when he is going to come at you.

If you are both in left fighting stance your opponent's leading hand is his left and your left hand is already halfway in position to stop the strike with the back of your hand which you must pull up to the side of your head. Keep the hand strong and open, but the fingers closed together. This is sufficient to prevent even a very fast back fist strike making contact with your head (photo 4:2).

Blocking a right-hand punch to the head

Most fighters naturally adopt a left stance in combat. This is because most people are right-handed and they feel comfortable using the left hand to deflect or block attacks, keeping the right hand pulled back,

4:1
Upper block: keep your head behind your arm for safety

ready to deliver the retaliatory punch. For this reason many left-hand back fist strikes are intended more as feints, preparatory to another stronger right-hand attack.

If a right-handed fighter changes stance and begins leading with his right foot and hand, he may be thinking of a right-hand back fist strike. In these circumstances you shouldn't let him settle and if you feel that he has such a move in mind with his 'better' hand, you should change your stance to match his. This will make it easier for you to block his right-hand attack.

If you don't change stance you are very open to his attack, since neither of your hands is in a good position to block it (photo 4:3).

4:3
In opposite stances it's difficult to block a back fist

4:2
Open hand block against back fist: not too near the head to give you control and a clear view

Blocking a roundhouse kick to the head

You may find yourself fighting a person who can do high roundhouse kicks, i.e. kicks to the side of your head. Let's look at the situation where you are both in left fighting stance, on guard and with left feet to the front. Your opponent attacks you with a roundhouse kick with his right foot to the left side of your head. To block this attack you raise your left arm from its front guard position to about 20 or 25 centimetres in front of your head and a similar distance to the side (photo 4:5). Keep the elbow pointing down towards the ground and the upper arm not quite vertical, but slightly inclined with the fist leaning towards your head.

The reason for the slight variation from the vertical is that, if you meet a kick at right angles with your wrist or forearm, you run the risk of a broken bone. The shin bone and foot are heavier and more muscular than your forearm and wrist and in a clash of bones the arm or the wrist will come off worse. However, if you incline the upper arm as it completes the block, the shin or foot will be more likely to slide away from the target, in this case in an upwards movement. This will result in your opponent involuntarily stretching his leg farther and higher than he can tolerate and he is likely to lose his balance. This will leave you free to attack him as you please, since his immediate thoughts will be directed at regaining his equilibrium before he falls over.

Make sure that your shoulder, arm and fist are tensed and ready to meet the force of several kilos flying through the air towards your head.

Another method of blocking such a kick to the head is to step back with the front, i.e. left, foot and block with your right hand in a sweeping motion from right to left across the front of your face (photo 4:6). Keep the hand open but the fingers closed (to prevent getting them caught in your opponent's trouser leg or wrenched back by the momentum of his attack), and simply stop

4:4
This back fist strike is clearly just a feint

the kick with your open hand, catching the lower shin and pushing it away from you to your left side. The kick must be interrupted by the block before it has gained too much momentum. This movement will take the impetus out of the attack and make your opponent drop his leg to the ground more quickly than he would like.

You must now act quickly and decide whether to make good your escape, since when he lands your back area and the back of your head will be exposed to an attack from his left hand. If you're quick and decisive you may wish to counter attack.

Reverse roundhouse kick defence

The reverse roundhouse kick is an attractive and powerful technique. When performed by an expert it is difficult to block effectively unless your reactions are very quick. The kick can be directed at your middle area, but is more usually targeted at the side of your head.

4:5
Blocking a roundhouse kick: arm not too close to the head, or your opponent may slip round your guard

4:6
When using reverse hand block early to smother the kick

The preparatory moves for this attack can be made without giving the defender much of a clue about what is to come. Your opponent's upper body can remain still and upright while he winds his hips round to swing his knee up and his leg round across the front of your body. When this happens your first move must be directed towards self preservation. In other words, move quickly backwards. By the time his foot is at its target it is full of power and you may be unable to block it effectively. So in this situation your blocking movement is secondary to moving out of range of the kick.

Assuming that you are both in left stance, your opponent's right leg swings across to make the attack. He may well have tried a feint punch to draw your attention from his real purpose. Additionally, if his feint is towards your face, his attacking arm may partially obscure your vision and you may not perceive his reverse roundhouse kick until it is already under way. You must act quickly and skip back. Don't step, as this takes more time. At the same time raise your left hand, open, and bring it across the front of your head to prevent the kick reaching you. Keep your hand open but your fingers closed tightly together (photo 4:7).

Don't use the back of your right hand or wrist, as you are unlikely to have sufficient strength in the arm to block effectively at that angle. Make sure that your block is a powerful one, which will completely ruin the attack and leave your opponent unable to follow up with any other technique. Another way is to jump into the kick. The attacker is vulnerable because he has turned his back.

Many reverse roundhouse kicks fail to score because of the difficulty of placing the foot accurately against the side of the head. Nevertheless, you should always be ready for the possibility of any attempt of this nature. It's better to jump smartly back than

4:7
Reverse roundhouse kick: block with your elbow down and hips twisted for leverage

to risk walking into a kick which, if successful, will score double points and could also upset your composure and feeling of stability.

Blocking middle area attacks

Attacks to your middle area, i.e. your chest, stomach area and your flanks, can come from either punches or kicks. We will deal with punches first. Again we start with both contestants in left free fight stance.

Outside arm block (soto ude uke)

As we have seen, it is usually your front (left) hand which does the defending and blocking, while the rear hand is the one which waits hidden behind to go through your opponent's guard and drive home your main technique. So we start with your opponent stepping forward with his right foot and punching you with his right fist as he completes his step forward. This technique, although powerful, tends to be slower in delivery than others, mainly because your opponent needs time to transfer his weight forwards and take his step.

You have a little more time to make your decision and perform the basic block in this technique.

As your opponent's right fist heads towards your chest, pivot on your front (left) foot, bringing your right foot all the way round behind your body until you are facing fully 90 degrees to the right. At the same time your front arm will open out to the left. As the punch starts to come into your body – or rather into where your body was at the beginning of your opponent's punch – your left arm swings in a short sharp movement to contact your opponent's arm with the flat underside of your wrist or the palm of your open hand. At the moment of contact you should twist your wrist in towards you so that your opponent's arm is diverted right off course.

If you can perfect the timing of this block it is possible to knock your opponent off balance, especially if you make contact and push him as he is completing his weight shift onto his front foot (photo 4:8).

Later, as your timing and confidence increase, you can try the technique with an open hand pushing your opponent's attack away across his own front. The advantage of the open hand is that you can control his movement more than you can with wrist-to-wrist contact.

In a competition you may be allowed to take hold of your opponent's clothing very quickly and briefly to assist in driving him across and away from you. You may not, however, keep a hold on him. Holds which lead to throws are permitted.

Inside arm block (uchi ude uke)

This is used in close contact where you find yourself with insufficient space and time to perform an outside arm block. It is done from the inside of the body and usually blocks your opponent's attack on the inside of his arm. It is a useful technique against a fighter who likes to swing punches round rather than drive them straight in as in traditional karate.

The point of contact is the sharp thumb edge of your wrist which should catch his wrist or lower arm just before it reaches its target (photo 4:9). In doing this technique it is recommended that you keep your fist closed. When close in with your opponent there is always the danger that with your fingers open you will catch them in the folds of clothing, your opponent's sleeve etc.

Double blocks

Once you have mastered the inside and outside arm blocks practise doing two blocks, one after the other. The reason for this is that you not infrequently meet fighters who like to attack with a double punch. Among the less experienced, this is usually in the form of a lead with the weaker fist, followed by a powerful second technique with the stronger hand. For example, your opponent may feint with an attack by his front hand, but he is really intending to draw your guard so that he can drive home a punch with his other hand through your exposed body defences. In order to defeat this tactic you should be able to perform a double block.

Double inside arm block

You and your opponent are standing in left free fight stance, with your left feet and left hands near each other. Your opponent slides his front foot forward and attempts a left punch towards your chest area. As this technique can be done quite quickly, you're unlikely to have time to move back sufficiently out of range. You must therefore rely on bringing up your right hand to do the block as you begin your rearward escape.

Your opponent, meanwhile, having tried to disturb your guard, then follows immediately with his main punch, which is a

❝ If all things were equal, a score against your middle area would be extremely difficult because you protect that area with both your arms. Once your opponent has drawn away that protection with a different attack or feint that equality ceases to exist and you become vulnerable to an attack to your middle. ❞

right-hand drive into your middle. Your reply to this is to bring your left hand quickly round and perform an inside arm block, effectively stopping his punch.

With practice, you will find that a double inside arm block done in this type of situation will leave your opponent's front exposed to counter attacking (photo 4:10), as your defending arms have driven both his punches out and away from his front area.

Outside and inside arm blocks
Your opponent comes rushing at you with, say, a right lunge punch, which he intends to follow with a left reverse punch. In this situation you have room to manoeuvre and you yourself move back and block the right punch with your left outside arm block. He follows up with a strong left hand punch to your chest, which you must now block

4:9
Inside arm block: the elbow is the pivot in a semi-circular movement

4:8
Outside arm block: a short sharp push sideways rather than straight down

---

POWER DRILL

★*Train for the inside arm block by making a short, quick step forward as you bring up your arm to parry the attack. It isn't necessary to unbalance your opponent, but merely to frustrate the flight of his punch.*

CHAMPION'S TIPS

● *Practise the arm movement first, then the body shift, then both together*

● *Don't waste energy with big, waving movements*

● *Avoid a chopping or swinging movement. Use the flat of the hand or the wrist to avoid hurting yourself*

4:10
A double block against a double punch will open up the attacker for a counter

immediately with your right inside arm block.

In this combination technique you should find that you have both stopped his attack reaching you and put him off balance, making it difficult for him to compose himself sufficiently to follow with any other effective technique. The reason is that his first right-hand punch has been blocked by you with your left arm pushing him across to his left front; your right-hand inside arm block has increased the momentum of his left/forward movement sufficiently to disturb his balance. His instinct will make him regain his own balance before he can think about another attack against you. This is the moment when you can turn the tables and counter attack.

Defence against kicks to the body
The front kick is a common technique. It is a powerful and intimidating kick. If you see a front kick coming and you have enough time, move immediately backwards or to the side, so that the kick does not land on its target. This is the most common form of defence against a front kick, mainly because it takes time for your opponent to shift the considerable weight involved and throw his leg in your direction.

However, you must be able to prevent a kick making contact with you if you cannot move out of the way.

Lower area block (*gedan barai*)
This is the most commonly used blocking technique against a front kick aimed at the stomach region. In this move the defending arm drives vigorously downwards to meet the oncoming lower shin of your opponent's attacking leg. The muscles of your arm must be strongly tensed and you must meet the leg at an angle which causes the leg to be deflected rather than at right angles. This is

CHAMPION'S TIP

● *There's a difference in technique between single and double blocks. In a double block you can't take the full benefit of body counter-rotation, which you do use in single blocks. To compromise you must strongly tense all your middle and trunk muscles as your blocks make contact.*

4:11
Lower area block:
sweep the leg across
and away from you

Variations in lower area blocking
You may find it difficult to use the basic lower area block if, for example, the kick is not delivered from directly in front of you or if it is made from close in or without warning. In these circumstances you will have to modify your technique to meet the threat. One of the most popular ways of deflecting a front kick is to sweep it and your attacker away from your body.

For instance, if you are both standing in left-front stance and your opponent kicks you with his right foot, you should skip – not step – back and with your left hand sweep the foot away from you by pushing it from your left to your right across your front. Keep your hand open and your fingers together. This is demonstrated in photo 4:11.

If you time this technique properly you will swing your opponent round to his left front and unbalance him. This will expose his right rib area and the right side of his head to a counter attack from you.

A spectacular defence against a front kick is to do a reverse right-hand sweep. As your opponent attacks you with his kick step forward and to his outside with your left foot. With a sweeping motion of your right hand drive your opponent and his leg even farther past you. As he is landing and recovering his balance you then seize the chance to turn and counter attack him before he can turn to pursue his own intended attack.

because the leg is stronger, heavier and more muscular than the arm and in a clash of bones the arm runs more risk of getting broken than the leg. Photo 4:12 shows the correct angle at which to meet the attack.

There is a slight, but essential, difference between the defences against punches and those against the front kick. Those where arm meets arm require firm contact bone to bone, but where an arm or wrist meet a shin bone the movement is much more of a deflection for obvious reasons. In other words you attempt to sweep a kick away from its target rather than risk a broken or injured arm by trying to stop it dead in mid swing.

4:12
Lower area block:
deflect the kick; don't
confront it straight on

Cross hands block (juji uke)

This requires a certain amount of courage to step in towards a kick which is aimed directly at your stomach. However, if you summon up that courage and you can see the kick beginning, you can bring it to a dead halt and again destroy your opponent's balance by frustrating his forward momentum.

Both of you are in left front stance. At the first sign of an impending front kick from your opponent, you step in, left foot still leading. Clench your fists tightly and cross them at the wrists. Your arms and body are tensed (photo 4:13). You catch your opponent's lower shin in the cross made by your hands while his leg is still bent and he hasn't yet got the full power into his thrust.

If you fail to block the kick properly or prevent his forward movement, however, your opponent may be able to follow with a punch, particularly to your face. In this situation you are open to attack, since both your hands are occupied blocking his kick. If your opponent is quick-witted he may catch you on the face with a punch before you can bring up your arms to defend yourself. Furthermore, your strong forward movement to block the attack will make it difficult

CHAMPION'S TIPS

● *Vary your blocks as much as you can*

● *Evasion is preferable to constant blocking*

to jump back out of the way if your opponent does follow with another attack.

Before your opponent can recover fully you should exploit the situation by following on quickly with one or two of your favourite techniques. Your favourite moves are likely to be the ones that you do well and so they are more likely to score and thereby increase your superiority over your opponent.

Body rotation

You may find it impossible to block or deflect a front kick. It may come too quickly for you to take evasive action or you may have misjudged your opponent's ability to reach you. Even at this advanced stage in your opponent's attack you may still be able to reduce the force of his kick, or even render it ineffective. This is done by turning your hips

4:13
Cross hand block: step in low, strong and purposeful

❛ The cross block is a very powerful technique and can protect you against heavy kicks and stick attacks. In traditional karate it is used in its open-hand form as a throat attack. Its use as an attacking move is forbidden in sport karate.❜

as the kick is coming into your stomach or chest.

To practise this move you and your opponent take up left fighting stance facing each other directly. Your opponent brings up his rear (right) foot to deliver a kick to your mid-section. As it is about to land you turn your body sharply and strongly to the right, using your hips as the pivot. The effect of this is that when your opponent's kick makes contact with your body, he no longer strikes you square on. Because the angle of impact has now changed, his kick will tend to glance off your body and he will be off balance to your right side. The more effective your turning movement the less likely will be your opponent to score on you (photos 4:14 and 4:15).

4:14
Turn your body to deflect the attack.

4:15
Body rotation: push the stomach out for strength

Attack and defence training

★ *You need a partner to practise this drill. You both take up left attacking stance. Number one attacker performs the right foot kick, just touching the side of his opponent's head. He then lowers his leg, with full control, back to the starting position. As soon as his foot is back on the floor number two performs the same move. As he finishes, number one then repeats his move and so on.*

Each should perform the technique five times before you both change stance and attack with the left foot. Once you can perform five of these adequately you can increase in stages to ten as you become fitter and more flexible. Don't take it to any more than ten as this will put an unnatural strain on your groin and muscles.

Don't push yourself beyond the pain barrier in any training where violent, wide sweeping leg stretching is involved. In repetitive training for the reverse roundhouse remember to place the sole of your foot against the target. As you become tired you must resist the easier way of just making contact with the point of your heel. This is not allowed and could be dangerous.

Turn the right way

It is important to ensure that in doing this technique you make the turn in the correct direction. If you are attacked by your opponent's right foot, turn to your right. If he attacks with the left, you must then swing round to your left. In this way your opponent is caught on the wrong foot and will find it difficult to follow on with a substitute attack, as he will be in an awkward position.

If you inadvertently turn the opposite way, you will find your opponent turning in towards you. He will have his rear fist ready to attack you as he comes in, but you on the other hand will find yourself facing away from him and unable either to defend yourself or counter attack him.

Stopping a roundhouse kick to the body

The roundhouse kick is one of karate's more popular – and also one of the strongest – fighting techniques.

The two target areas for the roundhouse kick to the body are the side/back area just above the hip bone, commonly known as the kidney area.

It is a spectacular technique and when performed correctly can score a full point in a contest.

It is also more difficult to target this kick correctly. The kick aimed at the kidney area often falls short or is delivered too low, usually onto the hip, which is worthless. Occasionally the kick goes too high and catches the shoulder, which isn't a vital area and is protected by a strong muscular structure around that area and so attracts no score.

Watch for warning signs

Many competitors, even quite experienced fighters, like to settle into a comfortable position before delivering a roundhouse kick.

It is the mark particularly of the lower grade to begin this kick after pulling back just a little from an opponent. He will often have both feet firmly on the ground and then raise his body as his rear hip rises and he starts to swing his leg out in a circle towards the side of your body. In karate terms, this gives you fair warning of his impending attack and your front hand should be prepared to spoil it (photo 4:16).

With more experienced fighters the circular movement of the attacking leg becomes less pronounced and also much quicker, which makes identification of the attack more difficult. However, as you yourself become more expert your reactions speed up and you should be more able to spot such an attack beginning.

Front kick lead-in

Many top fighters feint with a false attack which looks like the beginning of a front kick. Your opponent stands straight in front of you and his rear leg comes directly up towards you, knee high, looking just like a front kick heading straight for your stomach. Your natural reaction is to drop your guard, i.e. your front hand, to deflect this front kick. Too late you could discover that it was a trick and that the real attack is directed at the side of your body, for your opponent has suddenly twisted his hips and the kick swings round and hits you in your now unprotected area between your hip and shoulder.

Experience with different fighters will help you to identify this popular feint. You will find that people with very flexible legs and hips are more likely to employ this type of technique, while the stiffer stockier types are less inclined to use it.

★ *Practise this defence by hip-twisting as part of your warming-up exercises. When performing it in competition or general training keep your body upright and be on your toes so that you're as light and elusive as possible.*

' To score with a
good reverse
roundhouse kick is
a morale booster. If
you yourself are
scored on, don't
nurse your
wounded pride but
come straight back
into the attack. '

**Blocking a middle
area kick**:
4:16
Good anticipation by
the defender

4:17
Avoiding a kick to the
stance: step to the
side and drive your fist
down strongly

Blocking the middle area kick
Assume that you are both in left front stance. If your hands and arms are in a typical 'ready' position, that is with the elbows down, fairly close to the body (but not too close) and hands not any higher than shoulder level, you will find that the scoring area for a middle area roundhouse kick is fairly restricted.

As soon as you know, or perhaps sense, that a kick is on the way, draw down your left hand and arm to block the kick as it comes round to your left side. The nearer the instep you catch the kick the better, since if you catch it near the knee there may well still be enough power and leverage in it to drive your opponent's foot into your side in spite of your partial blocking of his leg. You can block with your fist closed or your hand open. If you use the open hand, which many prefer because it gives a feeling of more control over the block, make sure that your fingers are closed together (photo 4:16). Open fingers could be caught in your opponent's clothing and might dislocate or even break them.

Once you have successfully stopped an attack it is a good idea to move quickly backwards in case your attacker has it in mind to follow his kick with another technique.

Stopping a back kick

A back kick requires your opponent to be facing away from you as he performs it. The kick generally drives in towards you in a straight line towards your midriff. As with the reverse roundhouse kick defence, the ideal way out of danger is to move quickly backwards or to the side, mostly because you will be moving in line with the kick, but taking the sting out of it. The blocking part of your defence is done by the left hand making an outside arm block and sending the foot off to the side out of harm's way (photo 4:18).

4:18
Stopping a back kick: push the kick round and away as far as you can

COUNTERING ATTACKS

' Don't hesitate to counter attack. Don't let your opponent think that he's got you worried. Return the attack immediately so that you can get back on top.**'**

It will be apparent by now that there are three main methods of preventing your opponent's attack making contact and scoring. The first is to stop the attack from developing. The second is to remove yourself completely, or as far as possible, from the immediate danger zone. By these means your attacker fails to reach you and must then regain a fighting position to try again with another technique. There is invariably a moment during an attack when, if you have taken your evasive action, you should be able to counter attack. This moment usually comes when the attack is nearing its climax and your opponent is putting all his energy and concentration into the technique. This is the time to think quickly and take advantage of the situation by retaliating with an attack of your own. The type of attack to use depends on your opponent's movements and your relative positions.

The third way in which you can turn your opponent's scoring attempt into a chance for you to take the point is to use the blocking moves described in the previous chapter to manoeuvre your opponent into a position from which you can score and he cannot defend himself. Most blocks in karate are designed not only to stop or deflect attacks, but also to make it easy for the defender to counter attack.

Some people, especially when they are beginning karate, ask why they have to learn counter techniques which look slow and cumbersome compared with the speed and apparent ease with which their opponents can throw in a punch. The answer is that blocks and counters become second nature when practised regularly and they can be performed very quickly indeed once you have trained in them for a time.

A second reason for the great importance of blocks and counters is that most karate attacks don't actually score. This is due to incorrect timing, missing the target, not

5:1
Avoiding the head punch: protect and deflect with the left hand, punch under the ribs with your right

Opposite: A powerful straight punch from world heavyweight champion Vic Charles

Figure 7
Attack begins, defender about to take evasive action

Figure 8
Attack fails and the advantage is now with the defender

Countering a lunge punch:
5:2
The deflection is near the elbow; hold him off

5:3
Counter immediately with a hip turn and strong right punch

enough power, insufficient focus, a successful or partly successful block by the opponent and so on. So it's important not to shy away from attacks or to be satisfied merely with blocking them.

After an unsuccessful attack your opponent is for a split second vulnerable to a counter attack from you. Use that opportunity. When your instructor puts you into pairs to practise formal sparring techniques, remember that this is the reasoning behind it. Blocking and counter attacking is a fundamental part of karate and deserves as much time and attention as you can give it.

Evasions

Avoiding the head punch
A punch coming straight towards your head can often be deflected by your front, defending arm. Where you can't use this defence or you decide not to, your best avoidance technique is to move backwards or to the side! If you have enough confidence, you may move back just a little, or even merely lean your head and upper body back, keeping your feet planted in position. As your opponent's punch meets thin air instead of the chin he had hoped for he may begin to overbalance. At that moment he will start to regain control and either return to a fighting stance or begin a second attack. This is precisely when you have the opportunity to counter attack. As your opponent is aiming for your head, he

must raise his attacking arm and so leave his front and side chest area unprotected to a certain extent. This is the area you must counter attack. You must drop your body and drive in a right reverse punch to his middle area (photo 5:1, page 68).

Middle area evasion
It is more difficult to move away from a punch directed towards your chest because whereas your upper body is very flexible and you can move your head around comparatively easy, this is not so with your trunk. To shift the main part of your body you need practice to build up the necessary speed. Since you can't walk backwards as quickly as you can move forwards, it is not recommended to practise stepping backwards too much. It is faster to skip backwards or move to the side in avoidance techniques.

The sidestep
Sidestepping is a very useful move, since it can put you into a strong attacking position once your opponent's attempt has missed you. There are several variations of the sidestep but all work on the same principle. By changing the position of one or both feet, your middle area moves out of range of your opponent's attack.

For example, you're both in left fighting stance and your opponent attacks with a right lunge punch. As you see the punch, keep your front foot planted, but swing your rear, right foot to the left across your back until it is at the same distance and corresponding angle to the left of your own left foot. You'll find that the left foot remains in front and the right foot is still the rear foot, but your body has made a quarter turn to the right and in so doing has removed itself from your opponent's line of attack. The plan shows the position of the body and feet. Your opponent has totally committed his right fist and you're also out of range of his left fist. On the other hand you have the chance to punch your opponent on his exposed head or back rib area (figures 7 and 8).

The principle of sidestepping is also valid when facing a front kick. When using this defence, however, hold your arms ready for more defensive action in case your opponent has it in mind to follow the kick with a punch, particularly to your head.

If you decide to skip back rather than sidestep, remember to move smartly to your rear and cover plenty of ground. Many a front kick attack is followed by a punch and you must take yourself out of range of both these dangers.

It isn't very practicable to sidestep a roundhouse or reverse roundhouse kick since those techniques don't follow an easily identifiable predetermined route and don't travel in a straight line. With these techniques you must use the physical contact of your blocks to prevent them striking you.

Countering punches

It has been explained that many blocks in karate are designed so that, when performed properly, they position your opponent in such a way that he is vulnerable to a reciprocal attack from you. The main punching attacks to the head are the lunge punch, the reverse punch and the back fist strike. The descriptions of the moves in this chapter are all assuming that you are both in left fighting stance, i.e. left foot in front.

Countering a lunge punch to the head

When you see your partner's lunge punch coming at you, use your front hand to sweep

5:4

5:5

5:6

it off course. Once you have pushed him round and away from you you should seize the chance to attack his unprotected head or spinal region (photos 5:2 and 5:3).

Another counter attack is to step, not skip, backwards, which you may find time to do. As you step back with your left foot, drive up a rising block with your right hand and push the attack up and off to your right front. You have now opened up his chest area, which has no protection. Raise your front (right) foot and send a short roundhouse kick into his stomach. Make sure your kick strikes him above the belt to win your point (photo 5:6).

The third lunge punch counter attack is to catch the punch with your left hand and push it across to your right. The ideal spot is round about your opponent's elbow. At the same time you slide in, keeping your left foot in the lead, and punch up into your opponent's exposed right ribcage.

The reverse punch to the head counter

As with the lunge punch to your head, you almost always use your left hand, normally open (to give you more control) to deflect it across your front. Although many reverse punches to the face, especially by less experienced *karateka*, tend to fall short of their target, you can't take chances on this happening every time.

As you catch your attacker's fist and force it away you should use the opportunity to deal him a punch to the head with your right hand. You can also use the back of your left hand to drive the punch off to your left front. This has the effect of overbalancing your opponent to his right front area. In this situation he has little room for manoeuvre with his left fist and you should immediately follow up your deflecting block with a reverse punch into the chest area (photo 5:8).

Countering a lunge punch to the head:

5:4
Keep your opponent at a manageable distance

5:5
Raise the knee quickly for protection against a follow-up attack

5:6
Dig your kick in against his breastbone

Countering a reverse punch to the head:

5:7
Your upper arm and hand must be tensed. Use it as a cutting blade

5:8
Hip twist and punch in a straight line into his chest

CHAMPION'S TIP

● *A full power punch to your head will be followed immediately by your attacker's own head. As you counter, exercise control in avoiding hard contact on his face.*

CHAMPION'S TIP

● If you're unable to move your head away from a back fist strike, you may avoid being scored on by turning your head away from the attack. Although you won't prevent the strike, you'll change the position of the scoring area by taking away his target.

Countering a back fist strike to the head

As back fist strikes depend for effectiveness on speed and precision rather than power and drive, you are unlikely to disturb your opponent's balance in blocking one.

Such an attack is likely to come from either fist. When you are fighting someone who likes to attack with back fist strikes, note first which hand he prefers to use. If it's the left, leading hand your left hand should be on guard ready to slip up to meet an attack.

Don't block too soon in case he slides past your block and scores nevertheless. A back fist strike requires your opponent to reach out, leaving his left rib and chest area unprotected. As his arm comes over your guard you must drop your body, maintaining your left-hand guard. Then drive in a right reverse punch to his undefended body. You lower your stance for two reasons: to make your opponent's strike miss its target and also to give your punch better access to his body (photo 5:9).

Many fighters, especially the majority who are right-handed, often contrive to adopt a position where they can use a right back fist technique. In this case they will usually attack when their right foot is leading, as this will enable them to get more distance. If this happens to you, you can change stance and merely block and counter as above, but using the alternate hands. If, however, you find yourself still in left stance and your opponent is sending a right back fist towards your temple, your open left hand must come up and block it before it reaches your head. As you do so, again drop a little and counter attack with a right-handed reverse punch into the right rib cage.

Some less experienced fighters rely too much on back fist strikes and sometimes concentrate on them at the cost of developing a more varied selection of punches and kicks. If you meet such a fighter you should take the opportunity of practising the counter attacks described above. Learning how to drop your body and punch is very good practice for timing and focus.

Additionally, since many attempts at back fist strike don't score, either because they're not perfectly on target or are blocked, the counter attack has a good chance of taking the point. That is why it appears occasionally that a back fist, which was the first attack, doesn't get the score, whereas the defender's reverse punch counter attack, which came after the back fist strike, is awarded the point. So a back fist strike, although it may look impressive, is a gamble.

If you find yourself up against a back fist fighter, keep your composure, control his attacks and use these counters to help you win your bout.

5:9
Countering a back fist strike to the head: drop your body out of danger but use your hips to drive the punch into your opponent's left ribcage

The two main blocks against middle area punches are the outside arm block and the inside arm block and, occasionally, a downward block (*gedan barai*). Your left hand is the main defence against these punches. With a lunge punch or reverse punch you must ensure that you turn your opponent so that he is prevented from following with another attack to substitute for the one which has just been foiled.

Lunge punch to the middle area counter

If you decide to skip back, stop your opponent's technique with a left outside arm block, swing your block round to move him into a non-attacking position and punch him to the head with a left snap punch, followed immediately by a right-hand reverse punch to the body.

A second technique is to step back with your left foot and meet the punch with your left hand making a downward sweeping block (*gedan barai*). This movement will bring your opponent's body forwards and downwards, so that his head is brought into range for you to perform a fast right-hand back fist strike against his right temple (photo 5:10).

If you decide on the side step evasion, spoil the punch with a left-hand outside block and perform a right reverse punch to the side of your opponent's head. Once you've mastered this technique you can put in an extra punch. As soon as you've blocked his punch, bring back your left hand and use that fist to make a snap punch attack to your opponent's head, followed by your right-hand reverse punch, but this one now going into his right rib area. This technique done successfully in competition would attract a double score, since the two punches would be worth a point each.

Reverse punch to the middle area counter

You are both in left fighting stance and your opponent throws in a right-hand reverse punch towards your chest. Your left hand is your front-line defence. You should catch the punch, preferably with an open-hand block directed sideways. This will put your opponent off balance to the front and slightly to the right. You must counter immediately with your own right reverse punch to his middle area.

A second method is to block the punch with your right hand, at the same time using

5:10
Countering a lunge punch to the middle area: step back and block simultaneously. Follow immediately with the back fist strike

5:11
Countering a reverse punch to the middle area: not only can your opponent now reach you, but your kick has bent his body and he has lost his power

As with any attack coming into your body, it is vital that your stomach and chest muscles are tensed to meet the threat. Even a glancing blow from a front kick can wind you if your muscles are relaxed at the moment of impact.

Deflecting block
When your opponent's right foot kick comes at you, you sweep it off to your right with your left defending hand, as described in the previous chapter. As soon as you have removed the immediate danger you must counter attack. The two most obvious targets are the side or back of the head or the spine. The farther round you are able to swing him with your deflecting block, the more difficult it will be for your opponent to throw in a second, follow-up attack after his unsuccessful front kick.

Your counter should be a right-hand reverse punch. After your defensive swing to the right make full use of your returning hip movement to the left to produce a strong punch. If you are unable to swing your opponent's body far round, you can still attack his right rib area with your right reverse punch.

Reverse right-hand sweep
If you reverse the right-hand sweep there are two counter attacks you can use to score on your opponent. As you stride past him, you turn your body right round to face his back. You must turn right and not left. If you turn your body to the left you run the risk of walking into a back fist strike which your opponent is likely to throw on realizing that his kick has missed. A left turn means that you will be unable to see it. If you turn right not only will you have more warning of it, but you will have taken your head farther out of reach of his back fist. As soon as you have turned you can attack your opponent on his back or the back of his head. You must move quickly before he has time to turn round from his kick to face you.

The second counter attack is to use a back kick against your opponent's spine. As soon as you are clear of your opponent raise your right knee, look over your right shoulder to assess the distance and then drive your right heel into his unprotected back. This counter has the advantage of surprise and also protects your upper body from another immediate attack from your opponent. If your counter attack does not score it will

your left hand to go over the top of your opponent's attacking fist and deliver a left snap punch to his face.

The third counter to a reverse punch is to use a kick. Your legs are longer – and stronger – than your arms and if you see a reverse punch coming your way you should immediately kick your opponent in the stomach with a right foot front kick.

If you like, you can use your left foot; but remember that you have only a short distance in which to build up the power to make it a scoring technique and stop him in mid attack. Both these kicks should at least partially stop your opponent scoring on you because he will have been prevented from getting proper focus into his punch (photo 5:11). This technique is useful when there is a greater, rather than shorter, distance between you. Remember that when you are in punching range the punch will always get there first.

Countering kicks

Front kick defence and counter
As the front kick is one of the most powerful techniques in karate, your priority when being attacked with it is to ensure that it doesn't hit you. Or, if it does make contact, you should try to reduce its impact.

For example, if you take a kick in the stomach, turn your body to your right as your opponent's right foot is coming in. This will help to deflect the kick and make it glance off your body instead of making a direct hit.

keep your opponent at bay long enough for you to turn and face him again.

Kick for kick

There are two counter attacks in which you can use the front kick for retaliation. The first one is as follows. As your opponent comes forward with a front kick, you must skip backwards, maintaining your left foot in its leading position. As your opponent will have measured his kicking distance before beginning his technique, your moving to the rear will have taken his target out of range. As he lands on his leading foot, which is by now his right, you must move in to deliver your own right foot front kick into his stomach. Slide or skip in on your left foot to give you more speed and power.

The second counter attack using this kick is to step back as your opponent throws his kick towards you. However, you should step back only half a pace, to bring your left foot alongside your right. This move is sufficient to draw your body out of range of the kick from your opponent. As your feet come together you transfer the greater part of your body weight from your right foot onto your left. When your opponent's right foot lands close in front of you, having failed to reach you, you immediately return his attack with your own front kick from your right foot.

This technique is surprisingly fast. The reason is that a skip back is quicker than a full step back, because in a step back it is necessary to move the whole body weight a considerable distance to the rear. In the half-step backwards, however, the body is moved only a little, enough just to take it out of range of the kick and no more. This takes only a very short time and what looks like a defensive step backwards to avoid the front kick is in reality a preparatory move to attack your opponent with the same technique which he has used on you.

Look out for follow-up attacks

In all defences against front kicks you must keep your arms ready to block any second attack which your opponent may have ready in the event of his kick failing to score. Beginners will generally just try the front kick and no more. More experienced fighters will attempt to follow the kick with a punch in the form of a facial area snap punch, reverse punch or possibly a back fist strike.

If your opponent has attacked you with his right foot he may follow through with a right-hand attack. This is partly because it comes naturally with the way his body is balanced on landing after the kick, but also because you are out of range of his kick and he wants to reach you with his fist, which is easier with his leading hand. So remember to maintain your guard, particularly around your head, once you have avoided the front kick.

Experienced *karateka* can follow an unsuccessful front kick with any number of techniques. Among the favourites are a left-foot roundhouse kick, either to your middle area or to your head, and also a right roundhouse kick, which is done by pulling back the right foot after an unsuccessful front kick and twisting it round to make a roundhouse kick from the front foot.

You can't relax after deflecting or avoiding a front kick. Be on the lookout for what is coming next and either counter quickly to block the next attack or remove yourself speedily from it.

Counter attacking a roundhouse kick to the middle area

If you are both in left fighting stance, the angle at which you are standing could make you a suitable target for a right foot roundhouse kick to your left kidney area. The majority of such kicks are blocked by the leading hand, which you bring back and down to prevent the kick landing.

As the focus of your opponent's kick is your kidney area, your block will unbalance him a little. At that point you must lean in with your right hip and drive a right-hand reverse punch into his stomach. Because of the position of his body he will find it difficult to block your counter attack.

You may also find it difficult to reach your target because in a roundhouse kick the body often leans slightly away from the kick and the attacker's trunk may be out of range of a reverse punch counter. For this reason you must be ready to slide in, if necessary, to ensure that your punch gets home.

Less experienced *karateka* usually swing their kicks round as they attack, so giving more of a warning to the defender. With experience, they begin to make a tighter attack.

Don't commit yourself too much to a front kick defence. Try to keep your options open, particularly if you feel that the front kick is a testing technique rather than a full-blooded attack.

POWER DRILL

★ *Practise simultaneous blocking and counter punching against a middle area roundhouse kick. In front of a mirror perform together your side body block and the counter punch. When you've got the timing right train with a co-operative partner and turn it into a realistic counter move.*

5:12
Countering a roundhouse kick: you must drop right down and shoot your attacking leg behind your opponent's supporting limb

Counter attacking roundhouse kicks to the head

These are powerful techniques that can be countered successfully. They call for more effort than most karate techniques and so more commitment of your opponent's body. As soon as you see a roundhouse kick on the way you can use your hand to cover your head area and block the kick before it develops. With your other hand you should deliver a reverse punch into your opponent's chest area. Get the focus correct so that you can upset his balance while he is standing on one leg (photos 5:15 and 5:16).

In this counter technique you should practise punching your opponent with your right hand while your left hand is still up at your head as a block. You should also drop your body to improve your chances of avoiding the kick and also to increase your punching range.

Another counter to a roundhouse kick to the head is to step in with a left snap punch to the face as soon as the kick begins. Don't waste any time, but go straight towards your opponent's face. As he is concentrating on his kick and is balancing on one leg, his arms are partly concerned with helping to

maintain his balance. For these reasons a surprise snap punch can often get through to its target without too much difficulty. If your opponent is tall he may wait until you are a viable distance apart before he attacks you. If so, be prepared to slide in with your counter punch.

Disguised roundhouse attack counter
With experience, *karateka* modify and improve their techniques. Many fighters develop their own favourite methods of using roundhouse kicks. You will find a very popular ploy is to bring the knee up to the front as if to deliver a front kick. As your front hand drops to smother the expected attack to your stomach, your opponent's leg and body twist and you suddenly find that you are now facing a roundhouse kick at head level. When this happens you have to bring up your left arm and cover as much of your left side as possible.

Many a would-be attacker has suffered from the point of a defender's elbow jabbing into the top of his foot as he has tried to change his kick and bring a roundhouse up the side of his opponent's body. Using your elbow in such circumstances is not a recognized technique, but it can be very helpful in protecting you from a roundhouse kick.

5:13
Countering a roundhouse kick: as your opponent falls you rise and prepare for the finishing technique

5:14
Countering a roundhouse kick: the perfect finish to a spectacular counter attack

5:15
Countering a
roundhouse kick:
move in as soon as
your opponent's leg
comes out and round.
It is vital to maintain
your guard as you
move in under the
kick

5:16
Countering a
roundhouse kick: your
opponent has lost
control over his kick
and can't effectively
protect his stomach

Sacrifice counter

There is another counter to the roundhouse kick which is rarely seen in competition, but is very spectacular and will score a full point if properly applied. As your opponent's kick begins, you drop to the mat on your left rear side. Your right foot sweeps his left, supporting leg. He falls onto his back and you swing your right foot clear of him and deliver a kick with your right heel into his stomach.

It is a very unnerving counter attack for your opponent, who is being attacked from underneath where there is no protection. Your target area is your opponent's stomach (photos 5:12, 5:13 and 5:14).

It may look like a dangerous technique, but with control it's no more so than any other. Take care not to go anywhere near the groin.

Even if you don't succeed in scoring with this attempt, your opponent is bound to think twice about trying the next upper area roundhouse attack.

You shouldn't use this technique more than once or twice during a bout, however. If you do, your opponent will come to expect it, you'll lose the element of surprise and he can devise his own reply to your counter attack.

This counter is one in which you sacrifice your own stance and balance to secure the greater upset of your opponent's equilibrium and his ultimate defeat.

Countering a side kick

A side kick from the rear foot, although a little less popular in competition, is a strong technique, which relies on its power and straight thrust to get through one's guard and into the stomach and chest area.

This kick is difficult to deflect downwards because your opponent's strong thigh muscles are driving it forward. The best counter is to block it with a left-hand outside block and turn your opponent away so that you can counter attack his undefended head or spine (photo 5:17). The farther round you can spin your opponent the greater will be the expanse of his back which you can attack.

The head is the most obvious target. If you go for his head, make sure that your timing and focus are spot on. Making too much contact may incur a penalty against you: lack of distance or timing will not win you a point.

With his spinal region as your target you both have a larger target area, and also make

controlled contact with it, increasing your chances of winning the point.

The technique to use for this counter attack is the right reverse punch. Your left hand, ever on guard, must be up around your head area. The reason is that if your opponent is swung round properly his rotation becomes a spur to a right back fist strike against your head. If you block his strike with your raised left hand there is nothing else he can do to you at that moment. You now pick your target and push in a right-hand reverse punch, a technique which will earn you double points because of your opponent's exposure and complete lack of protection (photo 5:18).

Countering a side kick:
5:17
As you turn your opponent keep a wary eye on his front hand

5:18
Good timing and focus will earn a double score

TRIPS, SWEEPS AND THROWS

People love to see others being thrown in the air. It gives the performer of the throw a tremendous feeling of achievement, elation and personal satisfaction.

Balance is an important part of all sport. It is vitally important in combat sport, where to lose it or have it disturbed can lose a match. Although some people seem naturally to have more of it than others, good balance is not a matter of luck. Balance and how to use it for your advantage require a knowledge of certain principles.

Look at figure 9, which shows a stance with good balance. In this figure the body is facing forwards. The front foot is pointing very slightly inwards. It should never point outwards. The rear foot is directed more towards the front than the side. If the rear foot points out to the side there is no way in which the hips can be brought round to face

an opponent directly. The front and rear knees are bent slightly and the feet are not too close together, either longitudinally or laterally. The competitor is well balanced and will be difficult to push over or dislodge.

Figure 10 shows a weak stance. The feet lie almost in a straight line. Balance is weak to the right front and left rear, indicated by the dotted arrows. Additionally, the range of attacks is severely limited by the positioning of the body, as is the scope for self defence. The outward pointing front foot completes this almost suicidal stance. If the legs are straight then this competitor will be swept and scored against without having to move much more than a muscle.

Figure 11 demonstrates another example of weakness in stance. The feet are too wide apart and they are pointing outwards. This makes effective contact with the floor minimal. Only the heels are of any use, as the toes cannot grip the mat. This competitor is weak to the front and rear, indicated by the dotted arrows.

Obviously, if you kept to the ideal stance in karate you would not move very much and would be unlikely to score any points. But the principle of correct balance is clearly set out in figure 9 and it is the one in which you are least at risk from a tripping or throwing attack.

Avoid dangerous stances
Avoid standing with your feet in a straight line unless you have to. Practise also keeping the front foot under control. Don't let it slip or point outwards. As well as weakening your balance, your opponent will notice your clumsy steps and soon realize that you are ripe for a sweeping technique.

Another bad habit which the inexperienced *karateka* can fall into is to cross the legs while moving around the competition area. Crossed legs in karate is known as the 'position of sudden death'. With your legs crossed you can do nothing. If your opponent manages to sweep one of your legs he will undoubtedly sweep them both and you will find yourself sailing through the air and landing heavily. You will of course see high grade, experienced

Figure 9
A solid, well-balanced stance

Figure 10
A weak, unbalanced stance

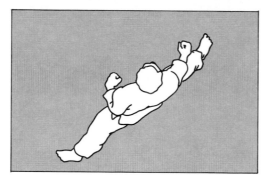

Figure 11
Unstable to the front and the rear

Opposite: The kick attack has failed and the defender is trying to upend his opponent.

12

Figure 12
A comfortable, well-balanced stance

Figure 13
A strong, balanced fighting position

fighters occasionally crossing their legs as they feint and weave during a bout, but they are fully in control and know exactly what they are doing.

As you learn to perform sweeps and throws and also how to avoid them, your balance will improve tremendously and you will automatically adopt safe and strong stances at all times.

CHAMPION'S TIP

● *Other combat sports in which balance plays an important part, for example judo, concentrate deeply on balance. In judo it's common for a competitor to make several body feints and diversionary push-pull moves to manoeuvre his opponent into a poorly-balanced stance and then throw him. The principle in karate is the same. For example, if you push your opponent back but then retreat yourself, your opponent's instinct will be to follow with hopes of hitting you. At that instant he's not thinking about balance and you'd be free to attempt a foot sweep on your unsuspecting victim.*

Correct use of the hips

When you decide to put your stationary opponent on the ground with a trip, sweep or throwing technique, it isn't enough just to use your leg. Before you is a person weighing many kilos. If you attack with merely the muscle power of your leg you are not likely to upset his balance with sufficient power to attain your objective. You must commit the bulk of your body to the attack.

When tripping with the inside of your right foot you assist the sweeping movement with a short but hard twist of your right hip. This will help to give power to your attack and to keep your own body properly balanced.

This is also the case with the short hooking movements which are a feature of some tripping techniques. For the bigger sweeps with the top edge of your foot the hips are also very important. With these techniques your whole body must swing in behind your attack.

A common fault is not to use the hip sufficiently, which results in a futile hacking movement at the opponent's feet. If your hips are flexible and you bring them round, helping to drive your sweeping leg right under your opponent's centre of gravity, you will certainly succeed in changing the position of his body from vertical to horizontal.

Centre of gravity and distance

Two key elements in techniques involving leg sweeps and take-down moves in general are the relative centres of gravity of the two fighters and the distance between the contestants at the time of the attack. When you are standing in 'ready' stance or in normal fighting stance, your centre of gravity is at a point just below your belt and is directly between the support formed by the position of your feet on the ground (see 'x' in figures 12, 13 and 14).

If however you lean your body too far in any direction, your centre of gravity moves so that it is no longer within the area covered by your supporting legs. In figure 12 the centre of gravity has moved in just such a manner and it is impossible for this person to prevent himself falling backwards.

Distance is also very important in your sweeping techniques. The farther you are from your opponent when you try to take his legs from under him, the more difficult it will be. You must be close enough to let your hips give you the power you need to pull his foot away with your own foot. If you are too far away you will find that by the time the driving power from your hips has reached your attacking foot, the energy in it has dissipated and all you can do is peck or hack uselessly at the lower end of your opponent's leg. If, on the other hand, you are too close to your opponent, you will have insufficient room to swing the hips and leg to make an effective technique.

Which foot to attack

Deciding which sweeping attack to use and which of your opponent's feet to aim for will come through experience.

When a person is standing in normal fighting stance his weight is more or less evenly distributed between his feet. Sometimes you may catch him, say, on his front foot when he has most of his weight on his back foot. In this situation he may go down to your sweep. But if almost all his weight is on his rear foot it will not matter that the support of his front foot has been taken away suddenly. His front foot will be knocked away and he'll simply resume his stance when your attempted sweep has failed.

Conversely, if almost all your opponent's weight is on his front foot and you attack that foot, you will have to find a great amount of drive and focus to take away this prop.

The ideal time to attack with a foot sweep

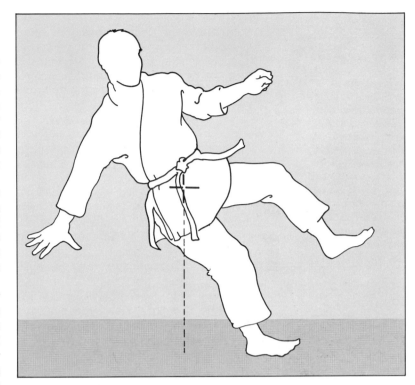

Figure 14
Past the point of no return

is when your opponent's foot has just begun to move or is just about to make contact with the floor. At those two points your opponent's foot, although not in full contact with the floor, is transferring weight either off that foot or onto it. If you can catch him at either of these two moments he will certainly go down.

There is a lot more to sweeping and tripping techniques than is immediately apparent. People who themselves have a low centre of gravity, perhaps being short and stocky, could do well with sweeps, since they can generate more power lower down when making their moves.

Follow-up techniques

Any take-down technique is not in itself sufficient to score a point. The theory of take-down techniques is that the fall is a way of putting your opponent on the floor and defenceless, for you to complete your attack with a punch or a kick from which he cannot escape. To score in this manner you must follow your take-down immediately with your main attack. If you hesitate you will not score. Even if you do a perfect punch, well-timed and with proper focus, you won't be awarded the point unless it follows your first technique immediately. If you are given the point for a good fast technique, you will be awarded double points.

Beware flailing arms

When people lose their balance, they often also momentarily lose their common sense. The first instinct when you feel yourself falling is somehow to compensate by waving your arms about with the irrational hope that by doing so you'll regain your balance. When you realize that this will not work your arms cease to try keeping you upright and they automatically drop to help your body meet the ground as gently as possible. Throughout this process, which takes only a fraction of a second, your arms will be flailing about in all directions. These things will happen to anyone you attack with a foot sweep, so it's important to keep your arms up in a protective position and to keep your head out of harm's way. Because there is a certain lack of control in your opponent's arm waving, he may in-advertently strike you. He won't score any points but he may injure you. So keep your guard up well around your head when you use leg sweeps in competition.

Sweep counter to lunge punch

Most counter attacks which use sweeping or throwing techniques are done when your opponent attacks with a kick. There is one technique, however, in which you can put your opponent down as he attacks with a lunge punch.

You're both in left fighting stance and your opponent attacks you with a right middle area punch. You must sidestep to the left, using your left hand as a back-up defence if necessary. As your opponent steps past you, use the instep of your left foot to sweep his right foot along and prevent it from landing. This will make him fall, since his weight, which has been transferred onto his front foot, now has nowhere to land and he will fall forwards with his front leg outstretched.

As with most foot sweeps, you attack the foot while it is moving and in the direction in which it is pointing. In this case you attack the rear heel of your opponent's foot and force it forward, not allowing it to stop or land (photo 6:1).

As he falls you must immediately punch whatever target area presents itself. Depending on the speed and direction of the fall, this will probably be the middle chest and stomach area. If you are extremely quick you may catch the back of his head with a right reverse punch as he goes on his way down.

6:1
Sweep counter to lunge punch: catch your opponent's foot just before it lands. Don't turn your own body too much

There are two areas of the foot which you use for sweeping and tripping techniques.

Instep sweep

The first is the soft part of the sole between the base of the large toe and the inner side of the heel. You point your toes and hold them tightly together and then turn your foot inwards. This movement makes your foot into a shape a little like a hook or spoon in which you can partially hold, say, the stem of your opponent's ankle or lower leg. If you make this shape properly you will find that neither you nor your opponent is hurt when you apply the sweep, even if you do it fairly strongly.

If, on the other hand, you don't have your foot in the right position and hack away at your opponent's ankles with your own ankle or the side of your foot, one or both of you will soon suffer pain and bruising, which would be quite unnecessary. The actual movement is one of brushing the floor with the outside edge of your foot. It isn't like a punch or a kick where you have a specific distance and target in your sight. Your sweeping movement stays and gathers up, as it were, your opponent's foot as it makes a sweeping drive along the floor (photo 6:2).

> ### CHAMPION'S TIPS
>
> ● *Slide the foot along the floor like a brush, using the outside edge*
>
> ● *The movement is an arc, not a straight line*
>
> ● *It is a sliding movement, not a kick*

6:2
Instep sweep: your leg is slightly bent, your body upright

6:3
Instep sweep: maintain contact between your foot and your opponent's until you're sure that he's fallen

❛There's little more exciting yet graceful in karate than to see a fighter drop to the floor in a spinning movement and lift his opponent off his feet and high into the air with a well-executed foot sweep.❜

Sweep with the top of the foot

The other method of sweeping is used in the more violent throwing techniques. It's done by pointing the toes of the attacking foot and keeping them tightly together to make the tendons of the top surface of the foot taut and strong. It's this part of the foot which makes the contact and breaks your opponent's balance. With this technique you usually attack your opponent's front leg. The movement is like, but not quite the same as, kicking a stationary football.

Keep your front (left) foot firmly planted on the floor to preserve your own balance and swing your pointed right foot round across the front of your body. You must keep the flight of your foot low so that it catches your opponent's foot around the heel or the outside area of his left foot. Don't catch him with your trip any higher than this, as you may bruise his lower leg if your sweep is too high.

On no account may you use this technique against the knee joint. Because of the 90-degree angle at which you make contact, there is the risk of dislocating your opponent's knee. If you are careless with this technique and catch the knee joint the referee could disqualify you.

Sweeping too high in any case lessens the efficiency of your technique because you are attacking an area nearer your opponent's centre of gravity. It is essential that you keep your sweep low to take him at the vulnerable point where his feet are in contact with the floor.

The balance and fighting ability of anyone, no matter how tall or small, heavy or light, depend completely on two small areas, only a few square centimetres, where the soles of the feet maintain contact with the floor. If you take away all, or some, of that contact area, gravity dictates that the body must fall to the ground. This is the principle on which foot sweeps work.

The top of the foot is also used in some techniques where you make a hooking movement to up-end your opponent. You attack the foot of your opponent with your straight, strong foot and on making contact turn your toes upwards and pull your foot up to make a cradle for your opponent's foot or heel. With this scooping movement you can control to a certain extent the direction in which you want to make your opponent fall.

The straight foot sweep and hook are pictured to show the difference between them (photos 6:5 and 6:6).

Front foot sweep

You are both in left fighting stance. You step up with your rear foot and use the inside sole to sweep away the leading foot of your opponent. To perform this technique while you are directly in front of your opponent is very difficult, because the ideal foot sweep takes the foot in the direction in which it is pointing. If you're standing right in front of your opponent this is clearly very difficult.

In a fighting situation, therefore, you wouldn't attempt this technique at that angle. You choose your moment when the angle is right, perhaps when you're side-stepping your opponent's attack or you find

6:4
Front foot sweep: keep your attacking foot low and your body tight and square

6:4

yourself at his left front. Now is the time for you to move. Brush the outside edge of your right foot along the floor to catch his foot at the heel. On making contact you must keep the movement going so that your opponent can't retrieve his foot and regain his balance (photo 6:4). With this attack your opponent will fall onto his left hip and left shoulder area. As soon as he does so you must put in your finishing technique. In this case it is a left reverse punch to the chest. Don't let your opponent slip away from you. Control him all the time.

There are many variations of this basic sweeping technique. As you become more proficient you'll acquire more flexibility in your legs and feet and you may not need to bring yourself round into the best position each time. With practice you can develop a hooking movement with your leg which will enable you to attack from less favourable positions.

Front foot inside sweep
This technique is a fast, surprise move calculated to upset your opponent's equilibrium and peace of mind rather than to put him on the floor.

You are both in left fighting stance. Your front feet are very near each other. You dart

6:5
Straight foot sweep: use hip turn to give impetus to your sweep. Don't come in too close

6:6
Straight foot hook: your knee is bent. Raise it as you press home your advantage

6:5

6:6

6:7
Rear foot sweep:
check the position of
your opponent's
landing feet before
you move in

6:8
Rear foot sweep:
guard against
retaliation from your
opponent's left fist as
you come in

6:9
Rear foot sweep: make
a strong sweep and
face your opponent as
he falls so that you are
ready for the finishing
punch

your front foot forward and scoop his foot on the inside surface, round about his inside ankle bone. You move your foot across your right front, which will send his foot out and towards his left front. If his feet are normally balanced your attack will upset him.

If your attack is a strong one he may be unable to retain control and he will go straight down. If he falls onto his front you must attack either his spine or the back of his head. If he turns during his fall, be ready with another follow-up attack, for example a punch into the chest.

If you don't succeed in putting him down, you should use this attack as a useful opening move for another attack, say a face or chest punch.

Rear foot sweep
This is a spectacular technique and one which will take your opponent by surprise. The opportunity for it comes when you find yourself behind your opponent. This moment usually comes when your opponent has attacked you with a roundhouse kick or side kick which has missed. As he lands, you move round behind him and sweep his rear leg with your right foot (photos 6:7 to 6:9).

To sweep an attacking front foot
The front lunge punch is a big technique which requires your opponent to step forward and go for the middle area or your head. Your guard should be up to protect your upper body. As he comes in you must sidestep and, keeping your guarding arm up against the attacking fist, sweep his right foot from behind. Catch him at the back of his heel and before his foot touches the ground.

If you catch him properly he'll collapse in a heap on the floor. As with all take-down techniques, ensure that you follow immediately with a scoring technique.

If you don't succeed in putting your opponent down, because you've mistimed your sweep, there is nothing lost. You're still in a good defensive position and you could well have found an opening for a compensatory reverse punch, for example, into his ribs.

Walking sweep
For this technique you walk from a position directly in front of your opponent towards your right front. You make a long step with your right foot as if to walk straight past him. Your left foot follows your right foot but,

6:10

CHAMPION'S TIP

● *If you're fighting a person who tries lots of foot sweeps you might try turning the tables on him. If he has to make many attempts he is clearly not very successful. As he sweeps your front foot lift it just enough to let his foot pass underneath. As he goes through, keep your own weight on your rear leg and sweep his attacking foot with your front foot. Keep your foot alongside his and, as he completes his movement and tries to put his foot back on the floor, force his foot further and lift it up into the air. He will overbalance and fall over. Look out for his arms waving about as he loses his balance*

instead of walking past, as your right foot has done, the toes curl up and make a hook. You turn up your foot and in the hollow at the top of your instep/bottom of your leg you catch your opponent's leg just above his foot. You then 'collect' his foot and drag it with you as you walk past. Again there is no backing or kicking movement at all. You simply catch the leg in an exaggerated walking movement (photo 6:10). Nor do you need much power. Your body and your balance are prepared for the move and it's your body weight which is the driving force behind the technique.

It's a great surprise to your opponent because the last thing he expects when you make such a move is to be falling forwards onto his face. He's more likely to be awaiting a back fist strike or some other attack to his left side.

As soon as you have pulled away his foot you must disengage your own foot and turn swiftly round left to deliver your scoring punch. This will normally be a right-hand reverse punch to the head or spinal area. As with most surprise techniques don't use this one too often.

Front kick take-down

In this technique your opponent attacks you with a front kick aimed at your stomach. As soon as you see what is happening you turn your body slightly to the left and block the kick with your left hand from inside. Then you step in, bringing your rear foot round to stand beside your front foot. You now pick up your opponent's kicking leg in the crook of your arm and with your right foot step

6:11

CHAMPION'S TIPS

● *Don't give the game away by making awkward preparatory manoeuvres*

● *Show your opponent your hands to make him watch them*

Walking sweep:
6:10
Make a positive walking movement past your opponent. Don't watch his feet

6:11
Immediately your opponent falls disengage your foot, turn and attack

through and behind your opponent's left leg.

For a technique such as this you are allowed to hold on to his jacket, preferably near the lapel, and lift him off the ground so that you can deposit him with control onto his back on the floor (photo 6:13).

The secret with this technique lies in taking control right from the start. You can't try a half-hearted attack: go straight in without hesitation. Step up and keep a tight and close hold on your opponent so that he can't escape and also so that he won't fall and injure himself. Keep hold of him until he reaches the ground. Remember that there is only you stopping him from collapsing heavily onto his back. So control his fall and when he lands he is completely at your mercy. You now pick your spot and immediately plunge a reverse punch right into his middle area.

Photo 6:13 is a good example of this well-executed technique. The defender has no protection and can't roll away. This technique will attract double points.

6:12
Front kick take-down: step straight in without hesitation

6:13
Front kick take down: keep a good grip as your opponent goes down so that he's not injured and you remain in control of his fall

**Reverse
roundhouse take-
down**:
6:14
Again move into your
opponent's body
without hesitating

6:15
Close contact on your
hip will give you
lifting power

6:16
A well-controlled
throw will demoralize
your opponent as
well as give you
an excellent scoring
opportunity

Reverse roundhouse take-down

As your opponent's reverse roundhouse kick is on the way up to strike you on the right side of the head, you slide forwards on your front foot and bring your rear foot round farther behind so that your body shifts nearer your opponent's centre of gravity. Turning slightly to the right, you thrust your right arm under your opponent's crooked leg at around the knee area. At the same time with your left foot you step past, but keeping very close to, his left foot, which is supporting his body and providing a fulcrum for his balance. As the kick reaches its peak you continue the lifting movement upwards, which is higher than your opponent had planned to go and will immediately off-balance him (photo 6:15). He is unable to hop out of trouble on his left leg because you have got your right foot behind it to foil any such movement. He must now over-balance. You continue your lifting movement with your right hand.

This technique, if not controlled, can drop your opponent onto his head. To prevent any accident, therefore, grasp his jacket around the neck area with your left hand and allow him to drop with some care into what will be an untidy collapse onto the floor. Your final move is to finish him off with a reverse punch onto the side or back of his head.

When proficient in this technique, you might try giving more excitement to the move by sweeping your opponent's left leg as you put him down. If you have lifted him properly with your right arm, much of his weight will already be taken away from his left foot, making a sweep considerably easier.

6:16

COMBINATION TECHNIQUES

'The single devastating attack is a rarity nowadays. The speed of modern karate and competition tactics demand a combination of two or more attacks.'

Single techniques can win the point if they are delivered with perfect, or near perfect, timing and with correct focus, but the reality of combat is that single attacks are usually countered successfully by an alert opponent. If you concentrate on single attacks your opponent will soon realize that all he has to do is block your technique and deliver a counter attack of his own choice.

Most attacks in karate matches consist of combination techniques, a series of two or more techniques delivered in succession. In basic form a combination attack is one in which you attack your opponent in such a manner that his guard is split between two successive and powerful techniques. Combination techniques are the essence of karate competition. They teach the *karateka* fluidity of movement, encourage versatility of thought and response and pressurize one's opponent into making mistakes, so opening the way for the attacker to win.

A combination technique which uses a feint is essentially a trap. You open your opponent up with one technique which he must block. You then attack the area, or areas, which are left unguarded.

Many combination attacks follow naturally from each other. For example, a right reverse punch will twist the hip like a coiled spring, which is all set for sudden release into a front kick or roundhouse attack.

Starting combination attacks
The transition from the practice of single techniques to combination attacks can be accomplished only if the basic moves themselves have been learnt properly.

When you do basic punching techniques you often leave the hand stretched out and tense for a split second to emphasize the power and timing in your technique. When performing in combination you must not do this. If you do, not only will you lose valuable time, but your opponent will also have the opportunity to take hold of your arm or leg and transfer the attacking initiative from you to himself.

Each constituent of a combination move must be practised individually. Don't skimp on the first attack. Don't say to yourself 'I don't expect to score with this punch, so I'll

just make a half-hearted attempt and save all my energy for the second technique'.

In a combination attack your first move is designed to score if your opponent fails to block correctly. If you do score with both techniques of your combination attack you will be awarded a full point, as long as the referee does not call a halt to the match before you can secure your second, follow-up point.

Types of combination
Combination techniques are in three groups: the punch/punch, the kick/kick and the kick/punch variations. The most common type is the kick/punch or punch/kick example. This is because to deliver two full-power techniques from the fists is more tiring and also more restricting in target areas, whereas the kick/punch variations allow more scope of attacking areas as well as spreading out the power required through the whole body.

Most combination techniques comprise just two, or less generally three, full-blooded attacking moves. Attempting any more than this vastly reduces the power and efficiency of each one of them, so that even if you are able to make contact with any of them, your lack of focus and strength would invalidate the attack and you would not score any points. Top international fighters have the two- or three-technique combinations in their repertoire.

Punching combinations

Snap punch/reverse punch
This technique is what is known in boxing as 'the old one-two'. You are both in left stance and you put in a left-hand snap punch to your opponent's face. Your technique will force your opponent to raise his front, left hand to deflect your fist across his face and away from him. As he is performing this action you must drop and drive in a right-hand reverse punch to his left chest area which is the part now left undefended by his left hand and arm.

Although a simple and fairly fundamental move, it is very popular. Beginners tend to make several mistakes when attempting this

Opposite: Perfect timing by the attacker who has completely opened up his opponent

POWER DRILL

★ *In front of a mirror practise the initial face punch with the second punch following in a flowing movement. In competition these two punches must come very close together. Use your practice time to blend them so that there's no gap when you use them in competition.*

technique. Among them are not making a strong enough push forward with the snap punch, with the result that the opponent's defending hand isn't really disturbed, and this in turn means that there is no gap into which the attacker can guide his follow-up reverse punch. Not using the hip sufficiently in the reverse punch and so not gaining the required distance is another common failing.

Variations

In spite of being a basic technique it is not as easy to master as it might look, partly because of these two common mistakes, and also because it is so popular that everyone expects it to be used at least several times during a bout.

Experienced fighters have developed their own particular styles and methods to turn this combination into a point scorer. A useful variation is to ensure that your opponent raises his defending hand sufficiently for you to score with your second punch by making a big forward slide of the body when you attack with the snap punch. At the same time make it look as though your right hand is also about to attack your opponent's face. If you come in hard and positively enough,

your opponent's instinctive reaction will be to raise both hands and arms to protect his head. If you succeed in drawing both his hands up in this manner, you will have the whole of his chest and stomach area to attack with your reverse punch.

Another variation which scores points is to attack the head with both punches. The trick in this technique is the way in which you deliver the first punch. When you throw the snap punch direct it not straight at your opponent's nose or the front of his face, but push it slightly off-target to your left, i.e. to the right side of your opponent's face. Your opponent will automatically draw his left hand across his face and block your technique. Since your punch has gone not straight onto his face but to the right side of his head, his hand will also have moved to the same position.

At that moment you must immediately follow with your reverse punch to the head. It is vital that you perform these two punches in quick succession, since you have only a fraction of a second in which to take advantage of your opponent's unguarded face.

Remember to direct your punch towards his chin area, so that if he turns his head up

7:1

Snap punch/reverse punch: make the punch realistic, but ensure that you don't reach your opponent

and back in an instinctive evasion you don't catch him on his upturning face and so lose by a penalty. Of course your initial snap punch must be realistic enough to force your opponent to adopt his hurried defensive block.

A further variation on this technique is to put in your initial snap punch from a stretching position, perhaps standing more upright than normal. If you judge your distance so that you don't quite reach your opponent with your left arm out straight, he will be lulled momentarily into a false sense of security (photo 7:1). You immediately take advantage of this by sliding forward on your front foot, so automatically dropping your body and centre of gravity, and force a right-hand reverse punch into your opponent's stomach area. Your opponent has mistakenly assumed that your out-stretched left arm marks the extent of your reach at that moment. Your drop and right hip turn demonstrate that in fact you have a far longer reach than was at first apparent (photo 7:2).

Back fist/reverse punch
This combination is also popular and is a good point-scoring technique. In this move

you substitute the back fist strike for the snap punch. There is, however, a significant difference in the stance that you adopt.

If your opponent is in normal left fighting stance, you must take up a right stance, that is leading with your right foot. Your first attack is a right back fist strike against your opponent's right temple, aided by a slide in from your front foot if necessary. Your opponent will have to block with his left hand, since that is his normal defending hand and he doesn't have time to bring his right hand up and round to do this job. In so doing, your opponent has to twist his body to the right, which in turn reduces his ability to counter attack with his right hand. Now it's your opportunity to take the point by putting in a strong left reverse punch to your opponent's centre or left chest area.

If you were to try this combination technique while you were both in left stance, your back fist strike would be more quickly blocked and your stretching movement would leave you vulnerable to a right reverse punch counter attack from an alert adversary. Performing the technique in opposite stances increases your own chances of scoring a hit while at the same time minimizing those of your opponent.

CHAMPION'S TIP

● In the back fist/reverse punch combination remember that you don't have to strike your opponent's front to score. Contact on the left or right ribcage is also a valid scoring point.

7:2
Snap punch/reverse punch: keep your body low, chin in, but head upright

Reverse punch/back fist:
7:3
Choose a good stance and draw your opponent's defending hand to you

7:4
Turn your hips to the right, throw in your back fist, at the same time removing your body from your opponent's line of attack

Reverse punch/back fist

This technique can also be employed in reverse, i.e. attacking with a reverse punch first, followed by the back fist strike.

If you use this method you must choose a time when you are both in the same stance, say left foot forward. On throwing forward your right reverse punch, drop your body. This gives you extra reach and also reduces your opponent's counter attack possibilities by partially removing your chest area. As you deliver the punch bring back your left hand, not to its usual position on your hip, but up over your right arm and shoulder to make a closed fist beside your right jaw and ear area. With your left elbow pointing towards your opponent your face area is well protected from any punch which he may contemplate throwing in that direction (photo 7:3). Your opponent has got to use his left hand to block your reverse punch, which is coming in under his guard because you have lowered your body. Immediately his left hand comes down withdraw your right fist and throw forward your left fist in a back-hand strike against his left temple. Your body must also come up at the same time to give added speed and reach to this surprise attack (photo 7:4).

Double reverse punch

The combination techniques described previously don't call for the attacker to step forward. The double reverse punch forces your opponent to move backwards as you push in with your second punch.

You're both in left fighting stance. You throw up a right reverse punch to your opponent's face. Instead of aiming for his lower facial area you put it straight in front of his eyes and momentarily hold it there. From this position and with your right arm straight you walk forward. As your right fist closes in on your opponent's face he will have to move back and prepare or begin his counter attack, almost certainly a right reverse punch. You continue your forward movement, but change direction so that you step past the outside of your opponent's front (left) foot. Not until you have almost completed this step do you pull away your right hand from in front of his face, where it has been obstructing his view. As you land you drive in a left reverse punch to the middle or left chest area.

The reason for moving to the outside of your opponent is that his counter punch will be directed at where he thinks your chest is.

He knows that you are coming forward, but because your right fist is obscuring his vision he doesn't know that you've moved into position on his left side and so his straight right punch will miss you.

When performing this technique remember to drop as you come in for your left punch to improve your access to his left chest area.

The double reverse punch is not very difficult to learn in its basic form. It is potentially an extremely useful technique. It is uncomplicated yet it scores time and again in competition at all levels. Anyone who likes punching techniques should practise this faithfully and develop his own method by experimenting with timing and body swerve to produce a successful attacking combination.

Train in this technique using both left and right stances so that you can attack from either side.

A simple triple attack

There's an easy version of the three-step punching combination, known as the 'triple', which is very effective.

It's done when you and your opponent are in left stance. You perform a right reverse punch to your opponent's middle area, dropping your body a little as you do so. Make a proper attempt so that he's forced to block it with his defending hand. When he does so, immediately withdraw your fist and start to step forward with your right foot. Bring your right hand back over the top of your opponent's arm and swing it into a back fist strike against his right temple. The strike should coincide with the end of your step forward.

As your opponent has had to move backwards out of range of your attack, he should now be in position for your final attack, a left-hand reverse punch to the chest or stomach. Since your move forward has been a long step and has not been exceptionally fast, your opponent will also probably have stepped. This means that at the time you deliver your final punch, he is in right stance, with his right hand still blocking your back fist strike and his left hand pulled back. You, on the other hand, are clear to punch his front or right front area.

Practise this technique from left and right stances. Aim to eliminate all jerkiness from your movement. Your objective is to develop a flowing technique of three separate, but non-stop, full attacks.

Kicking combinations

Front kick/roundhouse kick

This is the simplest of all the kicking combinations when performed with alternate legs.

From left stance you aim a right front kick to your opponent's stomach. Make it a positive and strong attack, but give him time to see it coming so that he's encouraged to step back out of range. As he steps back your kick will fall short. As you land on your right leg your opponent will have changed to right stance on moving back. He's now in a favourable position for you to follow up with a left-foot roundhouse kick to his kidney area. When you come in with the front kick keep your hands up in front of you so that he can't counter your kick with a quick jab to the face. Additionally, keeping the hands in position will give him no clue as to your next move.

Practise this combination from both sides so that you can use it from either stance.

The second, slightly more difficult example of the front kick/roundhouse kick combination is to use the same foot for both techniques. This is faster than the stepping technique described above and is used against an opponent who skips or slides back in defence.

From left stance kick into your opponent's middle area. As he drops his left hand to sweep away your kick withdraw your foot and turn the hip so that you can transform your attack into a roundhouse kick against the left rear of your opponent. You've drawn his guard away from his left area which is exposed because he's still leading with his left.

At first you'll find yourself unable to withdraw your leg from the front and turn it immediately into a roundhouse. The lack of flexibility in your hips and the unusual balancing required will slow you down. You must therefore practise in stages. As you withdraw your kicking foot from the first attack make sure that you bring the knee back and drop the foot to the floor. Put only the ball of the foot onto the floor beside, or slightly to the right front of, your left supporting foot, which remains stationary and firmly planted.

The purpose of putting your right foot down is momentarily to regain your balance before thrusting it out and round to strike your opponent around his left kidney area.

Keep your balance
A front kick to the stomach followed by a roundhouse kick to the head is a very effective combination. As you increase your speed you should stop putting your attacking foot onto the floor between kicks. Withdraw your foot, keeping your knee up for height and protection and simply turn your hip and your leg into a roundhouse kick onto your opponent's side or head.

Power in both techniques
A common fault when performing this combination is to concentrate too much on the second kick and ignore the importance of the first attack which, as a result, degenerates into a feint. As with all combinations, you must make your opponent believe that you are attacking seriously with your first move. Indeed, if you succeed you'll be awarded a half point for the front kick. If you also go on to score with the second kick, you may well be awarded a full point. Make both your attacks strong and forceful.

All competitors expect this combination to be used on them during a match. The secret of scoring with it is to be better at it than your opponent realizes. One of the most successful methods is to attack strongly with the front kick and then pause fractionally before beginning to withdraw the foot. This gives your opponent the mistaken impression that you had only got the single attack in mind. He will then momentarily relax with relief and think about a counter attack against you. At that moment you must twist round into your roundhouse kick which should be delivered as strongly as the first kick.

Roundhouse kick/foot sweep

There are several variations of this attractive technique. All of them attack first the head and then the other end of the body, which is the ideal method of upsetting balance, since the defender has to think first of defending his head before immediately transferring his concentration all the way down to his feet.

You are both in left fighting stance. Bring up your right leg in a strong and deliberate roundhouse kick to the head. Take it right up to the target and make your opponent block it. As he's had enough warning of your kick, he should feel safe enough to step back and build a greater distance between himself and the threat of your kick. When your kick is spent retrieve your leg and step down so that your right foot is in front. As you land make sure that your hands are up in front of you to spoil any counter attack, especially a left reverse punch, which your opponent may throw your way. On touching the floor transfer your weight onto the front foot and turn your hips to the right, bringing your left foot round in a sweep to take his right foot away from under him. As he falls keep close to him. Keep your own balance and as he lands punch him with a right reverse hand into his chest.

Variations
Many experienced fighters are reluctant to step back when attacked. They prefer to skip back just enough to keep them out of trouble. In this way they are ready to counter attack sooner after delivery of the round-house kick. If you meet a fighter like this and have found out by testing him that he regularly skips back rather than stepping, you'll have to vary your method of attack.

The first variation begins with your right kick to the head as before. As your opponent blocks it and slides back, withdraw your right foot and, without putting it onto the ground, drive your right hip and leg round to sweep your opponent's left foot away. Keep your foot tense and your toes pointed. If your opponent is very heavy or difficult to move you could hook the back of his ankle in your own right foot for added strength.

When starting to practise this technique you can drop your right foot to the floor to regain your balance and build up the power needed to sweep your opponent. Make sure that you land outside your opponent's front foot. If you land inside the foot you yourself may find your left foot swept or a right reverse punch hitting you in mid-section.

Another variation is useful against someone with a high stance. As in the previous technique, draw your opponent's hands up to his head by attacking it with a round-house kick from your leading, left foot. If you find it difficult to reach the head at short range, attack his chest instead. As he blocks, immediately drop your left foot to the floor at or near the position from which you started the kick. At the same time bring your right leg hard round and sweep your opponent's right leg, strong and low. Make sure that the movement is a driving one and not a kick. Your opponent should land on his back in a position where you will be able to deliver a clean punch to win you double points. A good example of this technique is shown on page 13.

Front kick/side kick
In this combination you attack your opponent's stomach with a strong front kick, keeping your hands up and in front of you. As he blocks or deflects the kick, bring the foot back to the floor and swivel right on the ball of the foot. As you turn, still with your hands up, raise your left knee and drive a left side kick into your opponent's middle area.

If you find it difficult to produce the second kick, it's probably because you haven't brought the front leg back far enough to get lift and strength into your left leg.

Roundhouse kick/side kick
This combination is more difficult than the preceding attacks, as it needs great flexibility of the hips. The attacker has to make a complete and speedy change of direction in hip rotation. In addition, the two kicks are completely different: a circular, snapping movement followed by a straight, thrusting attack.

Direct your right roundhouse kick onto your opponent's head or kidney area. When he blocks bring your foot back to the ground a short distance to your right front. Keep your body quite tight and don't place your foot too far out, since this will turn your chest into an easy target for a counter attack. As you land, lift your left hip and twist it to the right, keeping your knee up and your hands between you and your opponent. Opening up your hip, thrust the left foot deep into your opponent's stomach. Extend your leg fully and keep your head and upper body away from counter attack (photo 7:5, overleaf).

Roundhouse kick/back kick
This is one of the most difficult kicking combinations, but it's very powerful.

Attack your opponent's head with a roundhouse kick from your rear foot. Turn your hips and body as you do so and make sure that your upper area is out of reach of punches. As you land don't come round to face forwards, but continue with your turning movement so that your back is now almost towards your opponent. On regaining your balance, raise your left knee, look over your left shoulder and drive the left heel straight into your opponent's stomach.

In this technique your upper body leans right away from your opponent. This gives more leverage to the rear thrusting movement and removes your head from his punching hand.

CHAMPION'S TIP

● In the front kick/side kick combination keep the front kick at stomach level, then surprise your opponent by driving the second, side, kick hard into his chest area. His hands should still be at stomach level and he won't expect the more difficult kick to be put in higher up.

A common reason for the failure of this technique is that the degree of turn isn't sufficient and the attacker doesn't look over his shoulder to check that the kick is going the right way. Practise the turn in training sessions with your partner and always look over your shoulder to guide the kick to its target. If you follow these two rules you will produce a good finishing kick.

This technique can be used if your opponent is near the edge of the area, since the reaction to a kick coming in a straight line towards one's stomach is to move smartly backwards. If, in so doing, your opponent goes outside the area he may be penalized even if your technique doesn't actually score.

Combination hand and foot techniques

The number of variations of hand and foot combination attacks is virtually limitless. Some are relatively easy, others are difficult and taxing. Several joint hand and foot attacks are described below, which should give an insight into the principles behind them. Serious students can then develop their own variations.

Often when you perform a particular single technique, you find that your body is in such a position that it is poised to deliver a second, different attack. Some combinations of this type are described below.

Front kick/snap punch

You are facing your opponent in left stance. Raise your right leg, bent, and then straighten it as you kick into your opponent's middle area. Usually when performing combination techniques requiring a change of stance, the guard changes also, but not so in this example (photo 7:8). As you kick keep your guard up with the left hand leading. As you land a lot of momentum is produced in the right side of

Roundhouse kick/side kick
7:5
Your opponent may partially block your roundhouse kick . . .

7:6
. . . so you keep your balance as you retract your leg . . .

7:7
. . . and suddenly drive under his defence with a side kick

your body. Use that movement to drive in a right snap punch to your opponent's head (photo 7:9).

Begin the punching movement just before you land, so that you maximize the impetus of your forward body movement. In the perfect front kick/snap punch, the punch to the target coincides with the landing of the kicking foot onto the floor.

Beginners usually find the timing of this technique a little difficult. If you punch too soon you get only the forward movement of the body going into the punch, with no timing or focus. If you punch too late after landing you can get the timing and focus, but you have lost the power and the impetus provided by the body's forward movement. It is worthwhile spending a little time, preferably in front of a mirror, in getting this combination right.

CHAMPION'S TIPS

● *Hands should be still as the kick starts*

● *Hips straight as you deliver the kick*

● *Bring the leg back immediately after finishing the kick*

● *Stop any counter with your left hand*

7:8
Front kick/snap punch: cover distance with your kick but keep your upper body out of trouble

7:9
Front kick/snap punch: land square on with an immediate snap punch to the face

Roundhouse kick/reverse punch

In this combination you kick to the middle area or, preferably, to the head. Don't lean too far back with the kick, but just enough to keep yourself out of range of a snap punch counter. After delivering the kick, whether you score with it or not, bring the leg quickly back before you land with your right foot ahead, and to the right of, your left foot. Land square on rather than sideways, with your right foot outside your opponent's left foot. As you touch the ground use your already-turning hips to give force to your left

reverse punch into your opponent's chest. As you have landed outside his feet, you're in a better position to punch with your left fist than he is to retaliate with his right.

As you become more expert in delivering roundhouse kicks you can begin raising your knee quite high in front of you, between you and your opponent. This is to discourage him from attacking your middle area as you go into the attack. You should also try holding up your left hand (assuming that you are doing a left kick) in front of you as you kick to deflect your opponent's snap punch (photo 7:10).

This combination can also be changed round, with the reverse punch being used first.

As you attack with the punch you must cover extra distance, either by skipping or sliding in. Don't lean forward, which will overbalance you and invite your opponent to punch you on the face. When your arm is at full extension your right hip will be coiled and at this moment you loosen your roundhouse kick against your opponent's side. There should be no pause between the two techniques; they should flow from one into the other.

Reverse punch/reverse roundhouse kick

This technique requires good timing and a lot of hip turn, but is spectacular and can demoralize your opponent.

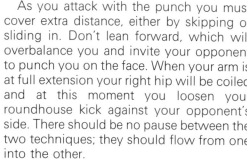

7:10
Roundhouse kick/reverse punch: push your leg out so that your opponent can't reach you

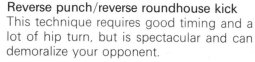

7:11
Roundhouse kick/reverse punch: use the downward momentum of your attacking leg to drive a right punch into your opponent's stomach

Manoeuvre yourself quite close to your opponent and suddenly make a reverse punch to his face. On this occasion put your fist right up to his eyes. This will make him blink and look momentarily at your fist and will also obscure his field of vision so that he can't see what you are preparing. As your punch is delivered wind your right hip round and bring up your right knee across your body between you and your opponent. As your foot goes up to deliver the attack against your opponent's head, withdraw your right hand and use it to help your balance.

A well-executed kick will attract a full point and even a reasonable attempt at this technique may also score.

Face punch/roundhouse kick/reverse punch

This technique is a strong attacking move which a defender finds difficulty in avoiding.

If your opponent is in left stance you adopt a right fighting stance. Step halfway up on your left foot, bringing it up beside your right. Turn your body a little sideways as you move up. This step is accompanied by a right-hand face punch against your opponent's head so that he can't fully see what you are doing. His left arm should move up to protect his head (photo 7:12). You follow this immediately with a foot roundhouse kick to your opponent's left kidney area (photo 7:13). By now he will have begun to move back out of trouble. Pursue him and attack him again before he is out of danger. On completion of your kick land with your right foot outside your opponent's left foot and give him a left reverse punch into the stomach (photo 7:14).

Practise this combination from both sides. For it to work to its best advantage, you must be in the opposite stance from your opponent. As with other combination attacks, each move must be strong and purposeful in its own right, yet must also be part of a smooth flowing pattern.

Face punch/roundhouse kick/reverse punch:
7:12
Not too close for the kick which is to follow

7:13
Note the defender's open scoring area

7:14
The defender is now too confused to counter effectively

SPARRING

There's no short cut to the top in karate. Regular sparring practice is essential for the successful fighter.

The two most efficient ways of training for competition in the *dojo* are the repetitive practice of basic techniques and pre-arranged sparring. Much of your karate club session will be taken up by these two activities.

As you all march up and down the floor doing a lunge punch or a complicated reverse roundhouse kick combination, for example, you are training for competition just as much as an elite international squad in their practice sessions. Only by constant practice, at least twice a week, can you master the basic techniques which will become second nature to you. You need to be able to call on them wherever you are, whether in the *dojo* or out on the street where you must defend yourself or some other person who is in danger. Unless your techniques are second nature to you, you will be unable to respond to the situation. So as you perform your techniques to the instructions of your coach you are building up a reserve of strength and expertise for yourself which you will be able to call on whenever and wherever it is required. If you are otherwise fit and healthy, do not give up or relax when you begin to get tired. You have to build up stamina and power, together with the correct performance of the techniques, to become a successful all-round karate competitor.

No-one can become a successful competition fighter without ample practice in pre-arranged and free sparring. Once the basic moves have been learnt, sparring is the bridge by which means the basic techniques are moulded and united with each other to make you into a good competitive karate fighter.

Pre-arranged sparring

Pre-arranged sparring (*yakusoku kumite*) is a highly important stage in the transition to competition fighting. There are two ways of training: one in the basic stances of the particular style you practise, the other in freestyle stance called *jiyu kumite*. Both are important in themselves, although the freestyle method is more directly relevant to competition.

At a basic level, you step forward and

attack your partner with a pre-arranged technique, say a lunge punch to the chest. Your partner responds by moving away, blocking and counter attacking. This is done at the command of the instructor and all the class members perform the technique simultaneously. The attacker will make, say, five attacks before the change round, when the erstwhile defender takes over the attack. This method allows each partner several chances to examine and improve his technique as he notices his mistakes.

Co-operation between partners is the essence of set sparring. You are not competing against each other. You are trying to perfect your own techniques while helping your partners to improve theirs. You attack and defend in turn, which is the best way to appreciate the give and take that occurs in karate competition. In pre-arranged sparring you can also practise some of the more dangerous techniques which are not allowed in competition. This widens your repertoire and also improves your overall reactions and appreciation of karate as a fighting art.

Aim for realism
Before beginning this training partners agree on what technique is going to be used, usually chosen in any case by the instructor. Since your partner knows what technique you are using, he is unlikely to be injured by something unexpected happening. When you attack you must do so strongly and not hang back. This is for your own good, to improve your technique, but is also necessary for your partner's sake. He also needs practice in defending himself against aggression and he can't do this if your attack is half-hearted or too soft. If you attack weakly your partner will easily dismiss your attack and will be denied the real feeling for the move.

Sometimes, because you know what defence your partner is going to use, you can unconsciously alter it to make it easier for him to block, or perhaps to make it less painful for you when he catches you on your wrist. The defender also knows what's coming and he should not anticipate the attack in any way. He should certainly not

Opposite: Sparring practice helps to produce strong and quick reactions

move before the attacker. At all times he should behave as though he doesn't know which attack is going to be used until it comes. He should then make his defensive move and counter attack.

Range and timing
Having agreed on the attack, defence and counter, you must consider range and timing. The correct range is the one at which the attacker would score on his opponent if the latter were not able to evade him. Beginners often stand too far away from each other, which means that both attack and defence fall short and are rendered useless. For punching techniques the ideal distance is generally about 15 centimetres between the two defending (front) fists.

There are several variables in determining distance, which include the height of the two partners and the depth of their stances. It is up to both participants to find their own optimum range.

Timing is an important part of competition training. Pre-arranged sparring is the best way for the attacker and the defender to improve their timing. As defender, you need as much warning as possible of an attack, so that you can render it harmless.

One way in which you can be sure that an attack is about to be launched is to observe your opponent's eyes closely. His eyes will very briefly narrow just before an attack. This is an instinctive movement and is an unmistakable warning that he's about to come at you. It doesn't happen if his move is a feint or not a genuine technique. In sparring practice the defender should look for this warning sign and put himself on maximum alert to move away when he sees it.

Sparring practice should start slowly, allowing ample opportunity for range and timing to be determined. Once you speed up the techniques and put power into them the defender should look for the eye-narrowing which precedes the main attack. In the flurry of competition it's usually impossible to identify this sign, but where you might have to defend yourself against an aggressor in the street it's a valuable help in establishing superiority in a violent situation.

Accommodating your partner
In this type of sparring the attacker should move at a speed which the defender can cope with. Some people are quicker learners than others; some find certain techniques more difficult than others. Some people have body co-ordination problems or have a physical disability. Everyone who trains in karate wants to learn the techniques and you should help your partner by not performing moves at a speed or in a way which he can't handle. As your partner's grasp of the move and counter-move improves, so you can increase the speed and force of the attack.

As the pace builds up the attacker and defender will often give out a loud shout called a *kiai*. It is a basic and strong shout resulting from the aggression built up and expressed as a person delivers his main technique. It is also used, more sparingly, in fights to give yourself courage and to intimidate the opponent.

The defender in set sparring must also show respect for the attacker. He should treat each attack as potentially dangerous and not relax because he knows that his partner isn't actually going to hit him. He could be wrong. So the attacker must allow the defender to improve his defence and the defender must treat each attack seriously.

Basic pre-arranged sparring
You and your partner face each other about three metres apart and perform the standing bow. Then both move into the ready position, usually left fighting stance. The club coach normally gives instructions and you perform all techniques exactly as he tells you.

If you are the attacker you step forward on the command and deliver your technique, say a lunge punch to the head. Your partner steps back and makes the appropriate block. Having successfully blocked your punch, he now puts in his own counter attack, in this case a right-hand reverse punch, perhaps accompanied by a *kiai* to assist his power and concentration.

At the end of the sequence you both move back into ready stance. Don't take your eyes off each other as you do so. Set sparring should be as close as possible to a real fight and it isn't unknown for someone who has apparently been defeated suddenly to spring up and turn the tables on his opponent.

Advanced pre-arranged sparring
As well as one-step sparring, most instructors teach three- and even five-step sparring (*sanbon kumite* and *gohon kumite*).

In a typical sequence the attacker drives a right front kick into the stomach of the defender, who slides back and deflects the kick across his body with his left hand (photo 8:1). On landing, the attacker pauses for a moment and follows with the same kick from the left foot. The defender steps back

' Sparring practice is particularly valuable when the partners are tired, for it is then that they tend to misjudge and make mistakes. This is comparable to the final seconds of a competition, when they must summon all their reserves and try to gain the ascendency. **,**

8:2

8:3

8:4

Advanced pre-arranged sparring:
8:1
A strong kick and equally strong block are necessary for realistic training

8:2
A straight punch to the undefended head: good practice for timing and distance

8:3
Force your opponent's hands up and his body back

8:4
With a powerful kick you draw your opponent's hands back down again to protect his stomach

and makes a similar block with the right hand.

If they are doing three-step sparring the attacker repeats his first right foot attack and the defender, sweeping away the kick, himself delivers his counter attack with a strong *kiai* to demonstrate his total concentration (photo 8:2). This form of sparring gives the attacker and defender experience of moving situations where they repeat the same attack or block, but in a changing environment where they must constantly adjust their range and direction.

In pre-arranged sparring the attacker should hold out the attacking fist or foot for a split second so that the defender can more easily define and perform his block and counter. As you become more proficient you should have less need to do so. In full competition you should never maintain your stance after your attack but withdraw at once in preparation for defence against the counter and your own follow-up technique.

CHAMPION'S TIP

● *Combination sparring is your chance to experiment with your techniques. You can judge your partner's reactions to your inventions. Use sparring time to try out your timing and direction of approach.*

Combination sparring

After training with single techniques, more complicated combination attacks are introduced in set sparring. The attacker can use his two or three moves and the defender has to nullify each one, finally delivering his own finishing blow.

A typical combination sequence would be you, the attacker, sliding into a left snap punch to the face, forcing the defender's head – and therefore his upper body also – up and back. As he skips back his stomach becomes a target for your right front kick. He must block this to survive. When he does so you withdraw your leg, swivel your hip, spinning on the ball of your left foot and make a right roundhouse kick against the side of your partner's head (photo 8:5). Your partner's left hand comes up again to block your kick. As you land drop to the outside of his front leg for your final attack, a left reverse punch to the body. Your partner really has to work now, because neither of his hands is in the ideal position to block your punch. So he makes his split-second judgement and blocks your punch with his right hand, at the same time delivering his own counter, a left-hand back fist strike to your left temple (photo 8:6).

Free sparring

This is the penultimate stage in karate. You and your partner can begin to regard each other as opponents. The techniques you use against each other are delivered at random by either of you at your discretion. Your attacks and defences are practised in a more realistic manner, but because of the random nature of the activity, many attacks may get through, so it is important not to punch or kick with full force. Attacks to the head must make very light contact at the most. The trunk of the body, which can absorb impact, can be attacked with more force.

If you have trained properly in pre-set sparring, you will have grasped the principles of fixing range and direction while on the move. In free sparring you develop this further by introducing the elements of opportunity and risk. You are at the same time attacker and defender.

In free sparring you aren't controlled by a referee and so you have to have your own conventions about when a point has been scored and when to stop. If you take an attack which penetrates your guard and makes good contact, you're expected to initiate a disengagement and make a small acknowledgement to your opponent that he

has scored. Many people make a small karate bow.

As free sparring techniques are more tightly controlled than they are in full competition, the defender should not take advantage of a 'pulled' attack by reacting in a manner or with a technique which would be disallowed or impossible in actual competition.

Freedom to experiment

In free sparring you are not bound by the strictures of the length of time for which you engage your opponent. You do not have to stop and return to the starting point every time a hit is made.

In theory there is no winner, although less experienced *karateka* often find this difficult to accept. They not infrequently try to 'win', as if something were at stake. This is not necessary, nor is it the purpose of free sparring. You free spar as part of karate training.

In free sparring you can try out your weaker techniques to make them better. You can experiment with new attacks and new stratagems. It doesn't matter if they aren't successful, since you lose nothing and gain in experience. By free sparring you can see what you are good at and you might be surprised. A technique you thought was one of your weaker points may be a viable one after all. Conversely, an attack which you imagined was one of your strengths may turn out not to be so successful in the hurly-burly of free sparring.

Free sparring is your opportunity to assess and re-assess your fighting ability and conduct. You can't do it in competition where you can't afford to experiment or do anything else but go out and win.

CHAMPION'S TIP

Protective equipment
● *In sparring practice it's permissible to wear extra protective padding. Fist mitts, shin and instep protectors, arm pads, head guards and even body armour may be worn at the discretion of your instructor or coach. This isn't only to soften the contact with your opponent, but it will also help to reduce bruising and abrasions on your body. Make sure your foot protector avoids your opponent's eyes as your kick passes his face*

8:5
Combination sparring: make full use of your hip turn to throw in a fast roundhouse kick to the head

8:6
Combination sparring: a difficult situation for the defender, who has only a split second in which to block the final technique and take the point with his own counter attack

COMPETITION

❝ The best
competitions are
those which start
and finish on time.
This requires good
organization, but
also needs the co-
operation of the
competitors. They
should not be late
for registration and
must be available
when they are
called to the
area. ❞

How competitions are run

This part of the chapter is necessarily brief and relevant to the aspiring fighter, since there are many rules and regulations, some of them complex, governing karate throughout the world.

Competition area

The area is a square, flat matted surface with eight-metre sides. Sometimes the availability of mats may necessitate a seven- or nine-metre square area.

Solid floors, whether of wood or some other unresilient material, should not be used, since they can cause injuries if fallen on awkwardly.

The area is marked out either in tape or the boundaries marked by different coloured mats. Around the perimeter there should be a one-metre deep 'escape area', which extends the safety margin outside the eight-metre mark. This whole zone must be kept clear of hazards and other impedimenta.

The competitors' starting points are on one-metre lines, usually taped onto the surface, each of them $1\frac{1}{2}$ metres from the centre of the area. The referee and judge start at points either side of the competitors, between the fighters and two metres from the centre of the competition zone (figure 15).

Match procedure

The referee calls the two competitors onto the area. To differentiate between them the fighter on the left of the referee wears a white belt and is referred to as *shiro* (Japanese for white) and the fighter on his right is called *aka* (Japanese for 'red') and wears a red belt. They bow on entering the area, take up position on their marks and bow to the referee and judge.

The match is begun by the referee calling *shobusanbon hajime* (three-point match begin). The referee and judge follow the fighters at right angles to them, keeping opposite each other so that between them they can see everything that happens.

When the referee wants to halt the match temporarily or bring it to a close he calls *yame* (stop). The match usually lasts for two or three minutes.

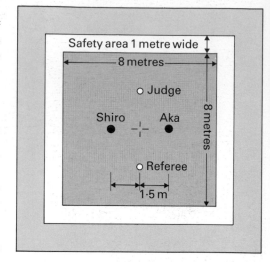

At the end of the bout the referee announces the winner by raising the appropriate arm above shoulder height in the direction of the victor. After this the contestants bow again to each other before leaving the area.

Referees and officials

The referee is the person in charge of the area and the one who runs the matches.

The judge assists him, standing opposite him on the other side of the fighters.

There is a third match official, the arbitrator, who sits on a chair just off the area, almost behind the referee. His job is to oversee the operation of the match and to make sure the rules are kept to. He also keeps a written note of the scores as they are awarded and may advise the referee, if requested, at the end of the bout.

These three officials wear a standard uniform of navy blue blazer, white shirt, official tie, grey trousers and dark shoes or slippers suitable for wear on the mat.

Two other people complete the total required to run a match: the official scorer and the timekeeper. The scorer keeps a written record of the score for the competition. The timekeeper is equipped with a stop-watch or clock. He stops the clock when the referee halts the match and restarts it as the referee continues the bout until the end of the aggregate time for the bout is reached. He gives a warning by bell or

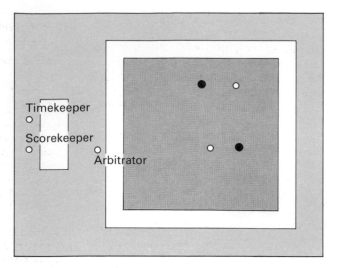

Figure 16
The mat officials move
around to maintain
close observation on
the fighters

buzzer when 30 seconds of the bout remain
and gives a longer ring to denote the end of
the match.

Figure 16 shows a typical example of the
positioning during a match. Between them
the referee and judge should be able to see
every move made by the contestants.

Scoring and penalties

Scoring

The winner is the competitor who has
scored most points by the end of the bout, or
the first one to reach the maximum of three
points called *ippons*, six half points or *waza-
ari* or a combination of both. In some styles
of competition the maximum score is only
one *ippon*, or two *waza-aris*.

Slightly imperfect techniques can be
awarded *waza-ari*. But some are given
ippon, such as any technique which is
delivered with, among other things, perfect
timing and focus, a good kick to the head, a

successful attack delivered at the precise
moment when your opponent attacks you, a
sweep followed immediately by a valid
follow-up technique, and also two or more
scoring techniques delivered in combination
before the referee calls *yame*.

The referee temporarily halts the match to
award the score and then immediately
restarts it with competitors and officials on
their original starting lines.

Penalties

Penalties are relative to the seriousness of
the infringement committed. For example,
the first instance of moving off the area or
inadvertently making slight facial contact
with an attack will merit a warning. A second
infringement of the same kind will earn a
penalty *waza-ari*, with the score going to
your opponent. A third similar offence will
lose you an *ippon*.

Other infringements which incur penalties
and even disqualification include using
forbidden techniques, attacking prohibited
areas of the body, reckless behaviour and
losing your temper.

For the repetition of a minor offence, the
penalty is called *keikoku*. A further repetition
merits the more serious *hansoku chui*. Yet
another repetition will lose the contestant
the bout through *hansoku*, which automatically gives full points to the other fighter.
Very serious offences can attract disqualification from the complete event or
competition *shikkaku*.

Imposing a penalty is always accompanied by the corresponding award of a
score to the other fighter.

If a fighter is unable to continue because
of injury, but not through the negligence of
his opponent, he will be retired and the bout

Figure 17
Waza ari to *shiro*

Figure 18
Ippon to *aka*

17

awarded to the other fighter. If the opponent culpably caused the injury, the result goes the other way.

Signals for scoring and penalties

The referee clearly signals points and penalties with his arms as well as calling out the point he has awarded.

For example, for a *waza-ari* he points with his straight arm and open hand about 45 degrees away from his body towards the competitor who has scored. To indicate *ippon* he raises his arm in a similar gesture, but above the level of his shoulder.

For *keikoku* he points with the index finger at the offender's feet; to indicate *hansoku chui* he points to the fighter's chest and for *hansoku* he points at the face. To indicate *jogai*, i.e. that a competitor has stepped outside the area, the referee points to the perimeter line behind the fighter concerned.

Some of these signals are shown in figures 17 to 20.

Team matches

There are usually five men or three women to a team, plus two reserves. Victory goes to the team which wins most individual bouts. If each team has an equal number of wins, the total points won by each side are added up to produce a winner. If that still results in a draw and a winner is needed, for example, to ensure that one of the teams goes through to the next round, a deciding bout is fought between a selected competitor from each team.

Weight categories and age limits

There are internationally-approved weight categories for karate competition. In a major official event, such as a continental or world championship, there are six weight categories for men: under 60 kilograms, under 65, under 70, under 75, under 80 and over 80 kilos, plus an open weight (that is, any weight). In female karate competition there are three weights: under 53 kilos, under 60 and over 60 kilos.

In *kata* events there are no weight limits for competitors.

In competition there is a minimum age of 18. Many official championships have a junior and senior section in the male events only. Juniors, which have the same divisions as senior men's, must be under 21: seniors are over 21. In response to the great increase in karate among teenagers, many countries have introduced under-18 competitions, which are strictly controlled for safety reasons and take into account a youngster's height and age as well as weight and grade.

Don't shoot the referee!

No karate competition, whether between two club mates on a training night or at a world championship, can take place without a referee to ensure that the competitors observe the rules. The pressures on a referee are as great as they are on the fighters. If a fighter makes a mistake, he may give away a point, or even lose the bout, but his performance is his own responsibility. If the referee makes an error he could cause the wrong person to win the bout. Many referees have been fighters themselves and understand very well the tensions and the difficulties of the competitors. All qualified referees are fair and competent. Those that are lacking in these two qualities are quickly identified and taken to task. If they do not improve, their federation or governing body

Figure 19
Keikoku against *shiro*

Figure 20
Hansoku chui against *aka*

A referee can't be all things to all people. He responds to what he sees. The more qualified and competent he is, the more likely his decisions are to be consistently sound and reasonable.

will certainly strip them of their qualification. When someone wins, the other person (perhaps your teammate) must lose. It is very convenient to dilute this unpalatable fact by attributing the loss partly to unsatisfactory refereeing.

While one cannot deny that all referees do make mistakes, they surely cannot be held responsible every time there is a loser in a karate bout!

A senior international official who has given refereeing courses in several countries begins his courses by explaining his four commandments.

'the right person should win'. This is the basic premise of all competition.

'every competitor should get what he deserves'. He means by this that officials should note transgressions and give penalties as well as awarding points.

'safety is essential'. Not all fighters have the same standards of personal conduct and recognition of safety regulations. The referee must ensure that fighters can compete absolutely fairly and evenly without undue risk of injury.

'the importance of presentation'. Referees should keep a high profile and control the match firmly but discreetly. They also have a great responsibility for enabling the fighters to get on with the match and for enabling the spectators to gain as much enjoyment from karate as possible.

These four thoughts get to the root of good refereeing and they represent the commitment of most referees in karate. So it is hardly fair to criticize the referee without good cause. His is a difficult, and often lonely, job.

Competition tactics

To become a successful competitor a *karateka* needs many things. One of the most important is the will to succeed and the will to win. To translate the basic techniques and combinations into success on the competition area requires dedication, patience and, very importantly, a good coach or club instructor.

Once you have reached the point of competing, it is useful to remember some basic points.

Anyone engaged in unarmed combat will almost invariably lead with his weaker hand. You must therefore keep one eye on your opponent's rear hand.

Watch your opponent at all times. Never let your attention wander even for a split second. Never turn your back on your opponent, even if you think you have scored a point or if your opponent is lying on the ground. Wait until you are absolutely sure that the match is over.

Easy, fast techniques are usually not very powerful. Powerful techniques require more preparation and strength than the shorter attacks.

Moving forwards is easier and quicker than going backwards. A skip is quicker than a step. Skipping forwards is fastest of all: stepping backwards is the slowest.

Do not stand sideways on to your opponent. This limits your range of techniques and renders your rear area vulnerable to attack. Never stand with your legs crossed, too close together or too wide apart.

Try to assess your opponent's breathing. If you can attack when he has just breathed out or while he is breathing in, you are more likely to overcome and break his body tension and thereby his resistance. A front kick delivered on your opponent's inward breath will wind him.

When you see a scoring chance, take it. Many fighters wait too long or put an attack off to await a better opportunity.

If you are ahead don't reduce pressure on your opponent. Build up the best lead you can and increase your reputation with the opponents you still have to meet.

If you are well in the lead you can try more spectacular techniques.

Vary your techniques so that your opponent doesn't know what to expect.

Use feints sparingly. They become obvious and your opponent will turn this to his advantage.

When you attack, your foot should always go to the outside of your opponent so that it's difficult for him to counter attack. Coming inside his front foot positions you ideally for him to punch you.

Make sure the referee can see your technique. A perfect punch or kick will not score if the person awarding the points is unsighted.

If you take a punch or kick and you aren't sure if the referee has seen the technique, there is no point in behaving as if your opponent has scored. Don't give the referee the impression that you have been hurt, or even hit.

Hints on kicking
When performing a mid-section kick, aim it high into the body. Your opponent will find

9:1

this more difficult to block. Front kicks can also be put into the left and right ribcage; these areas are also difficult to defend. Take care of your toes with front kicks. You can damage them if you do not pull them back fully. You can make more distance for your front kick by sliding forward on your supporting leg. Some fighters hop into the attack. Avoid too much kicking followed by stepping back, or your opponent will quickly realize that your front kicks are not very dangerous.

With kicking combinations it is better to attack the middle area first and then the head. An upper area kick uses a lot of power and energy and you may have little of both left if you kick first to the head.

A roundhouse kick from the front foot is very useful, particularly in combination with other techniques. It's also effective when delivered suddenly as a secondary technique when your first has failed. If you're flexible, a reverse roundhouse kick is a good opportunist move to confuse your opponent. Be careful to retain your balance on landing after this attack.

A back kick is more difficult to deliver in competition, but can be used, for example, against an opponent who is near the edge of the area. Use it to push him out so that he will be penalized. A side kick can be used for the same purpose. Open the hips, dig the supporting foot well into the floor to prevent your opponent turning the tables on you and pushing you over.

In competition kicks should start in as general and nondescript a way as possible. For example, bring the knee up in front of you to keep your opponent guessing. Are you going to proceed with a front kick, turn into a roundhouse kick, a side kick or spin round and drive a back kick into his stomach?

Foot sweeps
One of the main advantages of foot sweeps and trips is that even when they are not fully successful they destabilize the defender to some extent, which you can capitalize on.

A simple illustration is to attack the front leg with a right foot sweep, which will cause your opponent's guard to drop. You are then set up for a snap punch to his face. A high stance, or one that is too long, is an invitation to try a sweep. A double foot sweep would give you a strong psychological advantage. Attack the inside of your opponent's front foot with your front foot. He will probably not go down, but will apply

9:2

CHAMPION'S TIPS

● *Attack on your opponent's inward breath*

● *Attack when your opponent shows sign of inattention*

● *Attack when you think your opponent is going to attack*

● *Attack immediately the bout starts*

Foot sweeps:
9:1
Attack quickly and strongly, but maintain your own balance

9:2
The defender has helped to destabilize himself. Look out for his flailing arms as he falls

compensatory pressure in his lower leg against the push of your sweep (photo 9:1). Immediately return to the attack with a switch of foot and sweep him to the floor with a right foot attack to the outside of his front foot. The extra pressure applied by your opponent will help your sweep to put him down (photo 9:2). When he is down, remember to follow-up with a finishing technique.

9:3
Reverse punch: a good attack, but well caught and trapped

Punches

Snap punches are fast and relatively easy when practising, but be careful in competition not to make excessive contact in the hurly-burly of the match. You may be penalized, unless the referee decides that your opponent has contributed to the contact by walking onto your fist.

The back fist attack has a good reach and can be delivered speedily, but a high degree of precision is needed to score. Make sure that the referee can see your technique. It is no use if all he can see is your opponent's counter punch to your chest.

The reverse punch scores more points than any other technique. Top fighters develop their own styles and tricks of the trade to score with it. You should do the same. If you and your opponent are in the same stance you have only a fifty/fifty chance of scoring, because the defender's front hand is ideally placed for the block and his right hand well positioned for a reverse punch (photo 9:3). With the attacker now disadvantaged, the defender drives home his own reverse punch into his opponent's chest (photo 9:4). If you adopt the opposite stance to your opponent, you have a much better chance of scoring with a reverse punch by stepping outside his front foot as you punch with your left fist.

9:4
Countering a reverse punch: the counter attack must have timing and focus

Some medical facts

Injury

As a combat sport, karate is surprisingly free of serious injuries. Most injuries are superficial, such as cuts and bruises. The teeth often cut the inside of the cheek or lip when facial contact is too heavy. Less common are dislocations and, sometimes, fractures of the fingers and toes, particularly the thumb and big toe. More serious injuries are fortunately rare, but can include, for example, a broken forearm after blocking a kick, or a jaw injury following a head kick. Long-term injuries tend to show up as chronic joint problems, particularly of the elbow and knee.

Diet

You should have a normal, healthy diet, to include wholemeal bread and fresh fruit and vegetables. When in training you should merely take more of the same. Normally extra vitamins and minerals are of little value. On the day of a competition you should have a good fluid intake (as you will lose a lot during the matches) and not take a heavy meal within three hours of your first fight. Take small snacks and plenty of fluid during the day.

Drugs

The use of drugs is a controversial subject. Those which artificially improve performance are banned under international regulations and offenders are barred indefinitely from competitions. Some drugs, however, can usefully be taken during training under medical supervision. Anti-inflammatory and analgesic medicines can assist joint movement and help heal soft tissue damage.

Other drugs, such as cocaine, and even alcohol, can induce a feeling of confidence and well-being, but without any doubt they also reduce actual performance.

Anabolic steroids have only one beneficial effect. They help the muscles to recover more quickly after strenuous exercise and so they could enable an athlete to train harder. They do appear to have very serious side-effects and their use is, of course, banned. Additionally, their long-term disadvantages include the possibility of permanent sterility in males and the development of male characteristics in females; there is also a high risk of liver cancer.

Smoking interferes with breathing and its other dangers are well publicized.

The message of sports medicine experts is to observe the rules of common sense and to seek informed medical advice when in doubt.

General fitness training

New members of karate clubs often find it difficult to keep up with the class, since the exercises are new and the techniques look difficult. Fitness training for karate requires several ingredients. The most important elements are power, stamina and flexibility. These are built up of such factors as aerobic endurance and anaerobic endurance. Aerobic endurance is the ability to perform light, but prolonged activity; muscular endurance is hard muscular exercise continued until exhaustion sets in.

In other activities, such as marathon running and sprint swimming, the key training elements would be in different orders of priority from those in karate.

Strength is the ability of muscles to act against resistance. There are two types of muscle, known as fast twitch, and slow twitch. The former contract quickly, providing a lot of power in short bursts, and the latter provide more slowly, but for longer. Clearly, the short twitch muscles are more desirable for karate.

Speed is important because an attack has to reach its target in the shortest possible time. Additionally, reaction time is important in identifying and countering and attack.

Flexibility means the amount of movement in a joint. The more flexible a joint is, the greater will be the range of power and reach of a technique. In karate it is most important to ensure that the flexibility of a joint is linked with the ability of the muscles to sustain it. It is of little use having flexible hips enabling you to make high side kicks if your thigh muscles are incapable of holding the joint together when it is under stress. All karate clubs teach exercises designed to improve not only general fitness training but also specifically power, stamina and flexibility.

As you practise your karate, use this book to check your techniques, to give you ideas and guidance and to aid your understanding of the essence of karate.

CHAMPION'S TIP

Warm up and cool down

● *Cooling down after hard training is as important as the preparatory warm up. After training relax the muscles by performing gentle stretching and contraction exercises. This helps to expel the toxic acids which have built up in the muscles during the training session. If these acids aren't expelled you'll feel stiff and sore the next day.*

KATA

10:1
Note the long, deep stance of the knife hand block in the *shotokan* style

10:2
The same block in the *wado ryu* style: more upright, with a shorter stance

Opposite: Helen Raye, former double European champion in *kumite* and *kata*

As this book is concerned mainly with competition fighting, *kata* is discussed briefly and mainly in relationship with *kumite* (the fighting or combat aspect of karate) and general karate training.

Kata has no direct equivalent in English. It is the word used worldwide to describe a sequence of moves, blocks and counter attacks against imaginary opponents.

The study of *kata* helps the competitor to understand the fundamentals of karate. There is a certain discipline and a way of life attached to karate, which anyone who takes up the sport quickly comes to realize. The practice of *kata* is a method of expressing these feelings without having to fight an opponent in order to do so. *Kata* builds up stamina and confidence and it complements the one-to-one combat confrontation of *kumite*. A person who trains hard in *kata* is a good *karateka*, whether he is a successful fighter or not. Some people prefer *kata* to *kumite* and they make their full contribution to karate in this way as well as deriving great benefit from it.

Most *katas* take just a minute or so to perform, but they are nevertheless tiring, since they all demand complete concentration, full use of the body's strength and a high degree of flexibility. Moves in each *kata* are performed in a set sequence, must be performed in perfect timing and focus and take account of variation in speed.

All styles of karate have their own *katas* and *kata* competition is very popular at all levels. Many of the *katas* in one particular style have their equivalent in another style or styles. For example, the knife hand block used in Shotokan *katas* (photo 10:1) is depicted differently in the Wadu Ryu style, with a higher stance (photo 10:2).

Beginners in karate learn *kata* from an early stage, studying at first the very basic *katas*, which comprise two or three moves repeated in different directions and in varying positions. The moves in *kata* reflect the imaginary attacks by one or more opponents coming from different angles. As you progress up the karate ladder you have to learn more difficult katas. A black belt must know several set *katas* and be able to perform them to a high standard.

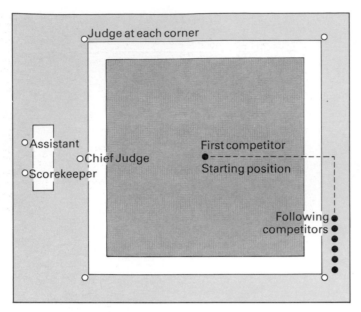

Figure 21
Plan for a *kata* competition

The combination moves in *kata* have been worked out very carefully by old karate masters and include many techniques which are too dangerous for competition karate. These include strikes, chops and kicks to vital areas as well as joint dislocation and techniques which break bones. *Kata*, therefore, is a useful means of studying and practising survival fighting techniques.

Kata competition

Kata reflects the traditional aspect of karate and the sense of discipline and *dojo* etiquette is very much in evidence. Karate suits must be clean, white and in a good state of repair. The five judges must wear the official uniform. The contestants come onto the area individually after making a collective bow to the judges. There is a strict format for the complete procedure, from how you enter the demonstration area to your withdrawal on the completion of your *kata*. As well as marking the *kata* itself, the judges will also include an element for etiquette in their scoring. At major *kata* competitions there are usually three elimination rounds, the last round is reduced to the final eight contestants. The winner is the person with the highest cumulative score.

Competitors must perform a different *kata* in each round, so no-one may repeat a *kata* in the competition. One judge sits at each corner of the area so that the performance can be observed with the optimum ac-

What kata moves mean

Moves in *kata* are given a practical application and it is important to know what the significance of each one is to perform the technique correctly. Photos 10:3 to 10:6 shows two moves from the *kata* Bassai Dai or Passai: the crescent kick (*mika geri*) is followed by an elbow strike (*empi uchi*) onto the opponent's chest or head. The practical application of this combination technique is shown in photos 10:7 and 10:8. The techniques used in *kata* are not confined to the attacks used in karate competition.

10:3
Focusing for a crescent kick in the *shotokan kata bassai dai*

10:4
The foot in mid-flight

10:5
The moment of contact. Note the well-balanced stance

10:6
A follow-up elbow strike

10:3

curacy. The chief judge sits at the head of the mat. All five of them award points individually and simultaneously (to avoid undue or inadvertent bias) at the command of the chief judge on completion of each individual *kata*. Behind the chief judge sits the score keeper and beside him his assistant, who is responsible for marshalling and identifying the competitors as well as ensuring that they appear in their correct order. Fig 21 shows the plan for a *kata* competition.

Individual and team competition

Kata competition for individuals is separated into male and female categories. There are also team *kata* competitions which operate under the same rules which apply to individuals. The team consists of three competitors. At international championships they are invariably all male or all female.

However some national *kata* championships sometimes feature mixed sex competitors.

10:7
The crescent kick would not only deflect the punch but could also break the attacker's arm

10:8
Practical application of the elbow strike. This devastating technique could easily break someone's jaw

10:6

GLOSSARY

This is a list of words most commonly used in karate. They are all Japanese.

Ai-uchi	simultaneous score (neither gets the point)	keri, geri	kick
aka	red (belt worn by one of the contestants in a bout)	kiai	karate shout
		kihon	basic techniques
ashi barai	leg sweep attack	ku	nine
bo	staff, long stick used in weapon training	kumite	sparring
		kyu	student grade, before reaching black belt
Budo	the way of martial arts	mae geri	front kick
chichi	seven	mawashi geri	roundhouse kick
chudan	mid-section (of the body)	mawatte	turn
dachi	stance	migi	right
dan	black belt grade	mubobi	penalty for failing to protect oneself
do	way, path		
dojo	training hall	ni	two
empi, enpi	elbow	nunchaku	rice flail, used in weapon training
encho-sen	extension to bout		
fukishin	judge	oi zuki	lunge punch
fumikomi	stamping kick	rei	karate bow
gedan	lower area (of the body)	roku	six
geri, keri	kick	sai	three-pronged fork, used in weapon training
gi	tunic, karate suit		
go	five	san	three
gohon kumite	five-step sparring	sanbon kumite	three-step sparring
gyaku zuki	reverse punch	seiken	fist
hachi	eight	seiza	kneeling posture
hai	yes	sensei	teacher, instructor
hajime	begin	shi	four
hansoku	foul	shihan	master
hansoku chui	warning of foul	shikkaku	disqualification
hantei	decision	shiro	white (belt colour of contestant in a bout)
hidari	left		
hiki-wake	draw	shobun	competition
hiza	knee	shobu ippon	one-point competition
ichi	one	soto ude uke	outside arm block
ippon	double points (literally, one complete point)	Taikyo ku	basic kata devised by Funakoshi
		te	hand
ippon kumite	one-step sparring	tetsui	hammer fist
jiyu ippon kumite	semi-free one-step sparring	tokui (kata)	(kata) of one's own choice
jodan	upper area of the body	tsuzukite	continue (after a bout has been temporarily halted)
jogai	going out of the competition area		
		uchi ude uke	inside arm block
ju	ten	uke	block
juji uke	cross hands block	uraken	back fist strike
kachi (aka-no kach)	decision (red belt is the winner)	ushiro geri	back kick
		waza-ari	point (literally, half point)
kara-te	empty hand (also Chinese hand)	yame	stop
		yoi	ready
kata	training sequence	yoko	side
keikoku	half-point penalty	yoko geri	side kick

SOME USEFUL BACKGROUND INFORMATION

Some karate styles

Shotokan — this style has deep stances and strong, deliberate techniques. It was founded by Gichin Funakoshi

Wado Ryu — characterized by an upright stance and fast punches and kicks. It was founded by Hironori Ohtsuka

Uechi Ryu — an Okinawan style which concentrates on body strengthening and conditioning; founded by Kanbun Uechi

Shito Ryu — a style with short, powerful movements, founded by Kenwa Mabuni

Shukokai — a derivative of Shito Ryu, developed by Chojiro Tani and Shigeru Kimura

Goju Ryu — a style with high stances and an emphasis on muscle power and stamina; founded by Chojun Miyagi

Kyokushinkai — a style which allows full contact blows to the head and body; founded by Masutatsu Oyama

Coloured belts

The colour of a belt denotes the level of technical expertise which has been reached by a *karateka*. A beginner usually wears a white belt (occasionally a red belt), progressing by examinations called gradings to a yellow belt. Passing further grading examinations leads to belts which gradually darken in colour, from orange/green, blue/purple to brown. These grades are called *kyu* grades and begin at ninth or eighth *kyu* for the first white belt. The senior brown belt is first *kyu*, which is the highest student grade.

On passing the first black belt grading, a person loses his *kyu*/student status and acquires first *dan* qualification and he wears a black belt. After this come second and third *dan* and so on. There is usually a three- or four-month waiting period between *kyu* grading examinations. A first *dan* must wait two years before attempting second *dan*, a second *dan* three years for third *dan* and so on.

To gain a black belt usually takes four or five years, but this can vary with the student's ability, the number of times he trains each week and the rules and syllabus of his own karate association.

Dress

For the sake of safety and in keeping with the discipline and etiquette of karate, standard karate suits must normally be worn. Beginners may exceptionally be allowed to wear, say, a track suit for the first lesson or so, but should acquire a karate suit, or *gi* as it is known, as soon as possible. It is purpose-designed for toughness, resilience and freedom of movement, especially for kicks. Karate suits should always be clean and in a good state of repair. A respectable club will insist on a high standard of dress. Most karate suits are white, although some associations and clubs have different colours, for example black or, occasionally, some other brighter colour.

Personal hygiene and safety

Karate is a very tactile sport and the risk of injury from personal carelessness must be reduced as soon as possible. Long hair should be tied back. Necklaces which can swing out and catch a person's face should be removed, as should watches and bracelets. Rings which cannot be removed can be taped over. Finger and toenails should be short and harmless. Don't train in bare feet if you have a foot infection. Students should attend classes in a personally clean state and not give offence or embarrassment to their training partners.

Safety equipment

In competition men must wear a groin guard. Anyone who does not may be disqualified. A gumshield is also permitted. It can be a useful safety aid, as it dissipates the force of a blow to the face as well as protecting the teeth and gums. Make sure that it fits perfectly. Mitts (fist protectors) are also compulsory as they soften contact to the head and other vulnerable areas. They are not used to allow you to hit harder than you would without mitts. A hard punch to the head with mitts on can do a lot of damage to the brain, despite there being no apparent skin bruising on the outside surface.

At the discretion of the referee, shin and instep protectors may be worn. No competitor may wear spectacles, although contact lenses are usually permissible. Women may wear a white tee-shirt or vest under the jacket and suitable protective equipment for the chest. A sports brassiere is adequate for most women. The referee may bar anyone who in his opinion is a danger to himself or anyone else by virtue of his dress or other physical factors.

The use of weapons

Weapons do not appear in any sport karate syllabus and they are not part of general karate training. There are instructors who give weapon training, usually to senior grades who have acquired the discipline, self-restraint and maturity needed to practise this more dangerous aspect of the martial arts. In the wrong, or inexperienced, hands these weapons can seriously injure the user as well as one's opponent. They include the *nunchaku*, a rice flail comprising two batons joined by a length of chain and swung around the body to keep opponents at bay, to lash out and also to use as truncheons. The *bo* is a long staff used to block and counter by thrusting and striking. The *sai* is a three-pronged metal fork, used one in each hand to block and trap weapons and arms and to retaliate with stabbing and striking attacks. Only bona fide *karateka* should practise with these weapons. Their value lies mainly in the arm strengthening and timing practice which they provide.

A word of warning: any person found carrying these weapons or handling them without good reason may be liable to criminal prosecution.

INDEX